LIFE AND DEATH IN ISIS

HOW THE ISLAMIC STATE BUILDS ITS CALIPHATE

**Zeina Karam and
The Associated Press**

Mango Media
Miami
in collaboration with
The Associated Press

AP AP EDITIONS

AP Editions

Copyright © 2016 Associated Press. All rights reserved. This material may not be published, broadcast, rewritten or redistributed.

Published by Mango Media, Inc.
www.mangomedia.us

No part of this publication may be reproduced, distributed or transmitted in any form or by any means, without prior written permission.

This is a work of non-fiction adapted from articles and content by journalists of The Associated Press and published with permission.

Life and Death in Isis *How the Islamic State Builds Its Caliphate*

ISBN: 978-1-63353-313-4

Publisher's Note

AP Editions brings together stories and photographs by the professional journalists of The Associated Press.

These stories are presented in their original form and are intended to provide a snapshot of history as the moments occurred.

We hope you enjoy these selections from the front lines of newsgathering.

"They are brutal people. They can consider you an infidel for the simplest thing."

-- Bilal Abdullah,
resident of ISIS held village of Eski Mosul

Table of Contents

PREFACE 7
INTRODUCTION 11
NATION OF FEAR 15
INSIDE THE CALIPHATE 37
BEHEAD THE DOLL 51
FLIGHT OR FIGHT? 71
STRANGER THAN FICTION 79
MEDIA WARS 97
CAPTIVE 115
THE ALLURE OF THE ISLAMIC STATE 129
WOMEN OF THE ISLAMIC STATE 145
COMING HOME 163
CHILDREN ARE THE FUTURE 179
CHRONOLOGY 193
CITATIONS AND BYLINES 199

PREFACE

On June 10, 2014, much of the world woke up to news that insurgents overran the northern Iraqi city of Mosul, rampaging through police stations, military bases and the airport in a stunning onslaught as security forces collapsed and fled their posts.

Within hours, the Iraqi army had lost control of the key city and black masked fighters with the Islamic State of Iraq and Syria (ISIS), an al-Qaida offshoot, were cruising through neighborhoods in pickup trucks mounted with anti-aircraft guns. Tens of thousands of Iraqi civilians fled in terror.

I was on a break in Switzerland when I received breaking news on my phone that ISIS seized Mosul. Confused, I called the Beirut bureau to check that I had not misunderstood. My instinct told me it was a watershed moment in the Middle East – and a precursor of major regional upheaval.

Less than three weeks later, the group declared the establishment of an Islamic state, or caliphate, in territories it controls in Iraq and Syria and demanded allegiance from Muslims worldwide. It declared Abu Bakr al-Baghdadi the leader of the new caliphate and renamed itself the "Islamic State" group.

Gripped, the world watched as the militants knocked down decades-old borders, effectively establishing a mini-state bridging Iraq and Syria, uniting a Sunni heartland across the center of the Mideast.

In the weeks and months that followed, people would ask themselves: Who are these people? Where did they come from? How were they allowed to become so strong?

For AP journalists in the region, covering the Islamic State group has been an exceptional time and challenge. Because of the high risk of abduction, we and other journalists are forced to report on the group from the outside. Shortly after taking over, the group cut off phone lines in Mosul and other areas under its control. The group also banned private Internet access in IS-controlled Syrian cities of Raqqa, Deir el-Zour and Aleppo, making any kind of reporting extremely difficult.

I had been covering the conflict in Syria since it started in March 2011, chronicling the country's spiral from peaceful protests to insurgency to brutal civil war. My colleagues and I had grown sadly accustomed to the endless stream of bad news and gruesome amateur videos of massacres.

Even that would not prepare us for the exceeding, much-publicized brutality of the Islamic State group, which took the violence to a new level, distributing images of the militants beheading, crucifying, burning and drowning opponents.

Syria's bloody civil war and Iraq's sectarian turmoil took a back seat to IS mayhem.

Covering the Islamic State means waking up in the middle of the night to report on videos of beheadings — some of them of Western journalists and aid workers abducted by the group in the summer of 2014. It means sifting through terrifying videos on social media every day and reporting people's stories about murder and rape.

On a trip to southern Turkey in March 2015, I interviewed many Syrians who had fled IS territory. Despite their fear, they were eager to talk about their life under IS even though most people had lost any hope that the world would help them. They shared intimate details about how they cope under a regime that extends its control into every corner of life.

My colleagues, Baghdad bureau chief Vivian Salama and Irbil video journalist Bram Janssen traveled many times to refugee camps in Iraq's Kurdish region as well as several towns in northern Iraq where some residents were just emerging from nearly seven months under IS rule.

We reported about how the group systematically recruits teens and turns them into killers and suicide bombers, even training them on carrying out beheadings by practicing on dolls.

Much of our reporting focused on the culture that the Islamic State group has created in areas under its control. Raqqa, for instance, a once-colorful, cosmopolitan provincial capital, was quickly transformed into the Islamic State's defacto capital where the group imposed its radical interpretation of Islamic law. Asked to describe life in the city, one resident chose one word: "Black."

In Islamic State-controlled areas, women must be entirely covered in black, and wear only flat-soled shoes. Black flags hang in main squares and black banners are plastered on buildings. Music is banned.

Armed members of the Hisba patrol, or vice police, patrol the streets, cruising in SUVs in search of any infraction. Women are chastised for being improperly covered and men who wear Western clothes or hairstyles are hauled off for interrogation or a lashing. Schools are segregated and curriculums have been changed.

People often vanish. Others suspected of being spies are hung from poles or shot in public squares.

While it imposes these suffocating measures on residents under its rule, the Islamic State group offers cash rewards and other incentives to its fighters. They are part of a generous welfare system the group has set up to help settle the thousands of jihadis who have flocked to IS territory from all over the world.

The U.S. formed a coalition in August 2014 and began launching airstrikes against the militants, which continue even now.

Despite some inroads, most observers agree that the global war against the Islamic State group has barely begun to scratch the surface. Under the Obama administration's campaign of bombing and training, which prohibits American troops from accompanying fighters into combat or directing airstrikes from the ground, it could take a decade or more to drive the Islamic State from its safe havens, they say.

Many Syrians and Iraqis told us they believe the Islamic State group will one day vanish just as quickly as it formed. Maybe it will, or maybe that's just one way of keeping hope.

Almost five years into their uprising against President Bashar Assad's rule, some Syrians say they now regret it ever happened, despairing of the violence it has unleashed across their country. Others are convinced it is Assad's brutality and conniving that allowed the group to flourish in the first place.

The Islamic State group is the result, among other things, of bad governance, sectarian politics and disaffected youth. It has thrived in the chaos of the Syrian civil war and Sunni discontent with the Shiite-dominated government in Iraq.

As long as such issues are not resolved, the group will continue spreading horrors across the Middle East, franchising in neighboring countries and threatening the West.

It is an ongoing, violent process to reshape the region, one that has touched off the gravest humanitarian crisis in the world today and contributed to the tide of migrants fleeing north to the safe shores of the European Union.

By Zeina Karam

Zeina Karam joined The Associated Press' Beirut bureau in 1996. She has reported on political upheaval, war and transformation in the Middle East for almost two decades. She was appointed bureau chief in April 2014, leading coverage of Lebanon as well as the devastating conflict in Syria. Karam is currently a member of AP's terror team and reports extensively on the Islamic State group in Syria and Iraq, April 8, 2014. (AP Photo/Hussein Malla)

INTRODUCTION

Demonstrators chant pro-Islamic State slogans as they carry the group's flags in front of the provincial government headquarters in Mosul, Iraq, June 16, 2014. (AP Photo)

WHAT'S IN A NAME? ISIS, ISLAMIC STATE AND MORE
Baghdad, Friday, September 12, 2014

Propaganda has been one of the core strategies of the Sunni militant group in Syria and Iraq that today calls itself the Islamic State - and its name is very much a part of that.

In July, the group's leader, Abu Bakr al-Baghdadi, announced its rebranding. He declared that the territory under his control would be part of a caliphate, or an Islamic state, shortening its name from Islamic State of Iraq and the Levant, or ISIL - the acronym used by the Obama administration and the British Foreign Office to this day. The Levant can refer to all countries bordering on the eastern Mediterranean, from Greece to Egypt.

Different translations for the name of the al-Qaida splinter group have emerged since the early days of its existence.

Some have chosen to call it the Islamic State of Iraq and Syria, or ISIS. The final word in Arabic - al-Sham - can be translated as Levant, Syria, or as Damascus.

Arab governments have long refrained from using Islamic State, instead referring to it by the Arabic acronym for its full original name, Daesh - short for Dawlat al-Islamiyah f'al-Iraq w Belaad al-Sham.

Several residents in Mosul, Iraq's second-largest city which fell to the extremist group in June, told The Associated Press that the militants threatened to cut the tongue of anyone who publicly used the acronym Daesh, instead of referring to the group by its full name, saying it shows defiance and disrespect. The residents spoke anonymously out of fear for their safety.

The inconsistency, while confusing for some, has not deterred the group's growing exposure on social media, with so many hashtags, posts and tweets ultimately directing readers and viewers to their news. Despite being associated to about a half-dozen names and acronyms, the group's brutal objectives are becoming increasingly clear.

Prior to the group's self-declared rebranding in July, The Associated Press opted to refer to it as the Islamic State of Iraq and the Levant, or ISIL, believing it was the most accurate translation.

The AP now uses phrases like "the Islamic State group," or "fighters from the Islamic State group," to avoid phrasing that sounds like they could be fighting for an internationally recognized state.

"The word 'state' implies a system of administration and governance," said David L. Phillips, the director of Peace-Building and Rights Program at Columbia University. "It's not a term that would be used to characterize a terrorist group or militia that is merely rolling up territory."

"Part of their strategy is to establish administration over lands that they control so that they demonstrate that they are more than just a fighting force," Phillips added. Equally problematic is the use of the word "Islamic" in its name, with some calling it blasphemous.

On Wednesday, French Foreign Minister Laurent Fabius referred to the group as Daesh, calling them "butchers" who do not represent Islam or a state. He urged others to do the same.

Egypt's top Islamic authority, Grand Mufti Ibrahim Negm, last month called on the international community to refer to the group as "al-Qaida separatists" and not the Islamic State.

"Their savage acts don't coincide with the name of Islam," said Sunni cleric Hameed Marouf Hameed, an official with Iraq's Sunni religious endowment. "They incite hatred, violence and killing and these acts have no place in any real Islamic state."

Chapter 1

NATION OF FEAR

Leader of the Islamic State group, Abu Bakr al-Baghdadi, delivering a sermon at a mosque in Iraq during his first public appearance, July 5, 2014. (AP Photo/Militant Video)

HOW ISLAMIC IS ISIS? NOT VERY
Cairo, Monday, March 2, 2015

    Three British schoolgirls believed to have gone to Syria to become "jihadi" brides. Three young men charged in New York with plotting to join the Islamic State group and carry out attacks on American soil. A masked, knife-wielding militant from London who is the face of terror in videos showing Western hostages beheaded.
    They are among tens of thousands of Muslims eager to pledge allegiance to the Islamic State group. An estimated 20,000 have streamed into the territory in Iraq and Syria where the group has

proclaimed what it calls a "caliphate" ruled by its often brutal version of Islamic law.

But how rooted in Islam is the ideology embraced by this group that has inspired so many to fight and die?

President Barack Obama has insisted the militants behind a brutal campaign of beheadings, kidnappings and enslavement are "not Islamic" and only use a veneer of Islam for their own ends. Obama's critics argue the extremists are intrinsically linked to Islam. Others insist their ideology has little connection to religion.

The group itself has assumed the mantle of Islam's earliest years, purporting to recreate the conquests and rule of the Prophet Muhammad and his successors. But in reality its ideology is a virulent vision all its own, one that its adherents have created by plucking selections from centuries of traditions.

The vast majority of Muslim clerics say the group cherry picks what it wants from Islam's holy book, the Quran, and from accounts of Muhammad's actions and sayings, known as the Hadith. It then misinterprets many of these, while ignoring everything in the texts that contradicts those hand-picked selections, these experts say.

The group's claim to adhere to the prophecy and example of Muhammad helps explain its appeal among young Muslim radicals eager to join its ranks. Much like Nazi Germany evoked a Teutonic past to inspire its followers, Islamic State propaganda almost romantically depicts its holy warriors as re-establishing the caliphate, contending that ideal of Islamic rule can come only through blood and warfare.

It maintains its worst brutalities - beheading captives, taking women and girls as sex slaves and burning to death a captured Jordanian pilot - only prove its purity in following what it contends is the prophet's example, a claim that appalls the majority of the world's 1.6 billion Muslims.

Writings by the group's clerics and ideologues and its English-language online magazine, Dabiq, are full of citations from Quranic verses, the Hadith and centuries of interpreters, mostly hard-liners.

But these are often taken far out of context, said Joas Wagemakers, an assistant professor of Islamic Studies at Radboud University Nijmegen in the Netherlands, who specializes in Islamic militant thought.

Muslim scholars throughout history have used texts in a "de-contextualized way" to suit their purposes, Wagemakers said. But the Islamic State goes "further than any other scholars have done. They represent the extreme," he said.

Militants of the Islamic State group with a captured pilot, Mu'ath Al-Kaseasbeh, wearing a white shirt, in Raqqa, Syria, December 24, 2014. (AP Photo/Militant Social Media)

It would be a mistake to conclude the Islamic State group's extremism is the "true Islam" that emerges from the Quran and Hadith, he added.

Despite its claim to the contrary, the Islamic State group is largely political, borne out of the conflicts in Syria and Iraq, said Khaled Abou El Fadl, an Islamic law scholar at the University of California, Los Angeles.

The group, he said, is trying to make God "a co-conspirator in a genocidal project."

Ahmed al-Dawoody, an assistant professor at the Institute for Islamic World Studies at Zayed University in Dubai, agreed.

The phenomenon of reading religious sources out of context "has existed throughout the ages," he said. "We should not grant any legitimacy to those who violate Islam, then hijack it and speak on its behalf."

"This is not Islamic terror, this is terror committed by Muslims," he said.

IS not only misreads the texts it cites, most clerics say, it also ignores Quranic verses and a long body of clerical scholarship requiring mercy, preservation of life and protection of innocents, and setting out rules of war - all of which are binding under Islamic Shariah law.

Many mainstream clerics compare the group to the Khawarij, an early sect that was so notorious for "takfir," or declaring other Muslims heretics for even simple sins, that it was rejected by the faith. The Islamic State group denies that, but it draws heavily from 20th-century theories of "takfir" developed by hard-liners.

Part of the problem in countering the group's ideology is that moderate clerics have struggled to come up with a cohesive, modern interpretation, especially of the Quranic verses connected to Muhammad's wars with his enemies.

Militants often point to the Quran's ninth sura, or chapter, which includes calls for Muslims to "fight polytheists wherever you find them" and to subdue Christians and Jews until they pay a tax. Moderate clerics counter that these verses are linked to specifics of the time and note other verses that say there is "no force in religion."

And while moderate clerics counter the Islamic State group's interpretation point-by-point, at times they accept the same tenets.

Sheikh Ahmed el-Tayeb - the grand imam of Egypt's Al-Azhar, one of Sunni Islam's most prestigious seats of learning - denounced the burning of the Jordanian pilot as a violation of Islam. But then he called for the perpetrators to be subjected to the same punishment that IS prescribes for those who "wage war on Islam" - crucifixion, death or the amputation of hands and legs.

This turns the debate into one over who has the authority to determine the "correct" interpretation of Islam's holy texts. Since many of the most prominent clerics in the Middle East are part of state-run institutions, militant supporters dismiss them as compromised and accommodating autocratic rulers.

The Islamic State group's segregation of the sexes, imposition of the veil on women, destruction of shrines it considers heretical, hatred of Shiites and condoning of punishments like lashings or worse are accepted by clerics in U.S.-allied Saudi Arabia, who follow the ultraconservative Wahhabi interpretation of Islam.

But IS goes further.

For example, most militaries in the era of Muhammad - the 7th century - beheaded enemies and enslaved populations they captured in war, including taking women as concubines. There are citations in the Hadith of Muhammad or his successors ordering beheadings, and verses in the Quran set out rules for dealing with slaves.

Ahmad Al-Tayeb, Grand Imam of Al-Azhar in Cairo, Egypt, June 4, 2015. (AP Photo/Mosa'ab Elshamy)

Pivoting off these, the Islamic State group contends that anyone who rejects beheadings or enslavement is not a real Muslim and has been corrupted by modern Western ideas.

One Islamic State cleric, Sheikh Hussein bin Mahmoud, wrote a vehement defense of beheadings after the killing of American journalist James Foley.

"Those who pervert Islam are not those who cut off the heads of disbelievers and terrorize them," he wrote, "but those who want (Islam) to be like Mandela or Gandhi, with no killing, no fighting, no blood or striking necks."

Islam, he wrote, is the religion "of battle, of cutting heads, of shedding blood."

To support beheadings, the group cites the Quran as calling on Muslims to "strike the necks" of their enemies. But other clerics counter the verse means Muslim fighters should swiftly kill enemies in the heat of battle, and is not a call to execute captives. Moreover, IS ignores the next part of the verse, which says Muslims should set prisoners of war free as an act of charity or for ransom.

The Islamic State group "appears to have adopted violent ideas first, then searched books of religious interpretation to find a cover for their actions," said Sheikh Hamadah Nassar, a cleric in the ultraconservative Salafi movement.

A photograph of James Foley, the freelance journalist killed by the IS group, is seen during a memorial service in Irbil, Iraq, August 24, 2014. (AP Photo/Marko Drobnjakovic)

In June 2014, the extremists declared a caliphate, or "khilafa" in Arabic, in the lands it controls in Iraq and Syria, with its leader Abu Bakr al-Baghdadi as the caliph - a declaration roundly ridiculed by Muslim clerics of all stripes. But here too, the group went further, saying that Islam requires the existence of a caliphate and anyone who refuses to recognize its declaration is not a true Muslim.

"The hopes of khilafa became an undeniable reality," the group proclaimed in its online magazine, Dabiq. Any Muslim who refuses IS authority will be "dealt with by the decisive law of Allah."

After that, the stream of IS recruits swelled by thousands.

BRUTAL PEOPLE
Eski Mosul, Iraq, Thursday, June 18, 2015

Inside the Islamic State's realm, the paper testifying that you have "repented" from your heretical past must be carried at all times. Many people laminate it just to be safe. It can mean the difference between life and death.

Bilal Abdullah learned that not long after the extremists took over his Iraqi village, Eski Mosul, a year ago. As he walked down the street, an Islamic State fighter in a pickup truck asked directions to a local mosque. When Abdullah didn't recognize the mosque's name, the fighter became suspicious.

"He told me my faith is weak and asked, 'Do you pray?'" Abdullah recalled. Then the fighter asked to see his "repentance card." Abdullah had been a policeman until the IS takeover, and policemen and soldiers are required to have one. So are many other former government loyalists or employees - even former English teachers, since they once taught a "forbidden" language and tailors of women's clothes because they once designed styles deemed un-Islamic.

Abdullah had left his card at home. Terrified, he sent his son running to get it.

"They are brutal people," he told The Associated Press. "They can consider you an infidel for the simplest thing."

Bilal Abdullah poses for a portrait in the village of Eski Mosul in northern Iraq, nearly a year after Islamic State militants took over the village, May 26, 2015. (AP Photo/Bram Janssen)

The Islamic State's "caliphate," declared a year ago, stretches across northern Syria through much of northern and western Iraq. Untold numbers have been killed because they were deemed dangerous to the IS, or insufficiently pious; 5-8 million endure a regime that has swiftly turned their world upside down, extending its control into every corner of life to enforce its own radical interpretation of Islamic law, or Shariah.

The Islamic State's domain is a place where men douse themselves with cologne to hide the odor of forbidden cigarettes; where taxi drivers or motorists usually play the IS radio station, since music can get a driver 10 lashes; where women must be entirely covered, in black, and in flat-soled shoes; where people are thrown to their deaths off buildings on suspicion of homosexuality; where shops must close during Muslim prayers, and everyone found outdoors must attend.

There is no safe way out. People vanish- their disappearance explained by a video of their beheading, an uninformative death certificate, or nothing at all.

"People hate them, but they've despaired, and they don't see anyone supporting them if they rise up," said a 28-year-old Syrian who asked to be identified only by the nickname he uses in political activism, Adnan, in order to protect his family still living under IS rule. "People feel that nobody is with them."

The AP interviewed more than 20 Iraqis and Syrians who survived life under the group's rule. One AP team travelled to several towns in northern Iraq, including Eski Mosul, north of Mosul, where residents are just emerging from nearly seven months under IS rule. Another AP team travelled to Turkish cities along the border, where Syrians who have fled IS territory have taken refuge.

What follows is based on their accounts, many of which were verified by multiple people, as well as on IS social media and broadcast operations and documents obtained by the AP, including copies of repentance cards, weapons inventories, leaflets detailing rules of women's dress and permission forms to travel outside IS territory - all emblazoned with the IS black banner and logo, "Caliphate in the path of the prophet."

The picture they paint suggests the Islamic State's territory, now an area roughly the size of Switzerland, has evolved into an entrenched pseudo-state, one based on a bureaucracy of terror.

The Takeover

In January 2014, when the Islamic State group took over the Syrian city of Raqqa, Adnan fled, fearing his work as a political activist would make him a target. But after a few months of missing his family, he returned to see whether he could endure life under the extremists.

Adnan found Raqqa transformed from a once-colorful cosmopolitan city into the Islamic State's de facto capital. Women covered head to toe in black scurried quickly to markets before rushing home, young men avoided the cafes they once frequented. IS fighters turned the city soccer stadium into a prison and interrogation center, known as "Point 11." One of the city's central plazas was now referred to by residents as "Jaheem" Square - Hell Square.

Fighters from the Islamic State group parade in Raqqa, north Syria, undated. (AP Photo/Militant Social Media)

He soon learned why. He heard celebratory gunshots one day and saw the bodies of three men dangling from poles in Hell Square. The corpses were left there for three days, he told AP as he chain-smoked in a cafe in Gaziantep, a town on the Turkish border filled with Syrians living in exile.

The reign of terror he had fled had gotten only worse, he said.

Each time the Islamic State group overruns a community, the pattern has been roughly similar, AP found - as methodical as it is bloody.

First comes an initial wave of killings of police and troops. Then the fighters often seek to garner support by quickly repairing electricity and water lines. They call on bureaucrats to return to work. Government employees and any former troops or policemen sign their "repentance" papers and must hand over their weapons or pay fines sometimes amounting to several thousand dollars.

In loudspeaker announcements, mosque sermons and leaflets, new regulations are laid out: No smoking, no alcohol, and no women working except as nurses or in women's clothing shops, where even mannequins in store windows are covered. Residents said they were required to build walls outside their homes so women would never be seen.

Militants from the Islamic State group leading away captured Iraqi soldiers dressed in plain clothes after taking over a base in Tikrit, June 14, 2014. (AP Photo/Militant Website)

In each district, an "emir" - often a local militant - is appointed to govern. Schools close, then reopen with IS-written curricula. Taxes are imposed on businesses. Pharmacies are given Shariah courses and banned from selling contraceptives. In most locations, tribes or families declare loyalty to the group and gain positions or perks, several interviewees told AP.

Adnan stayed in Raqqa for almost a year, watching the extremists pervade nearly every aspect of life. IS authorities came to his family's car parts store and demanded taxes - the equivalent of

$5,000. The group was clearly flush with money from taxing businesses, confiscating lands from those who fled and sales from oil fields captured further east in Syria, Adnan said.

The group encourages commerce across the "caliphate," he said - for example, cement supplies and vegetables moved from Turkey, through Raqqa to Mosul, Iraq's second-largest city

Then Adnan's one-time activism in support of Syrian rebels caught up with him. In January, a patrol raided his family home, confiscated his laptop and arrested him for publishing online articles they said encouraged secularism. "Such a pretty house," a patrol member said before smashing two glass water pipes. "This pollutes the environment," he told Adnan.

For the next 55 days, Adnan was held in Point 11, the soccer stadium.

He was interrogated three times in the initial days, beaten with a green plastic pipe. Then he was moved out of isolation into wards with other prisoners.

Soon after came another gruesome moment. One of the top Islamic State judges in the area, a local man known by the pseudonym Abu Ali al-Sharei, dropped by in early February to teach another lesson in Islamic law to the prisoners. He made small talk with a roomful of them. Then he grinned and said, "Listen, I haven't told you yet, but today we made al-Kaseasbeh crispy."

He took a flash drive out of his pocket, Adnan said, and, to the prisoners' horror, played them footage of captured Jordanian Air Force pilot Muath al-Kaseasbeh being burned alive in a cage by his IS captors.

Adnan's account is just one example of how IS uses the execution videos that it broadcasts to the world online to also intimidate people under its rule.

In Raqqa's prison, Adnan's job of distributing food to other inmates gave him a broad view of operations.

He saw two Kurdish prisoners and overheard wardens saying the pair would likely be used in Kurdish-language propaganda videos before being released. Adnan said he also saw several foreign Islamic State fighters being held - three Turks, an Uzbek, a Russian and a Yemeni - apparently on suspicion of spying. Two other IS fighters were brought in for stealing booty looted from the Syrian Kurdish town of Kobani rather than sharing it with other fighters.

Kobani was the scene of the biggest defeat of IS in Syria, when Kurdish forces backed by U.S. airstrikes drove off the militants after months of heavy fighting.

"We gave up 2,200 martyrs in Kobani, and you go and steal?" Adnan said he heard the interrogator shouting at the two detained militants.

Adnan met Palestinian prisoner Mohammed Musallam, whom IS accused of being a spy for Israel. Musallam told Adnan his captors were repeatedly filming him in his own execution video. Each time, he said, they would video a child shooting him in the head - but each time the gun would be empty.

"Then one day, they executed him for real," Adnan said.

In March, the Islamic State group released a video showing Musallam's death. Kneeling in a field, he is shot in the head by a young boy wearing military camouflage.

Adnan said he believes that is why many victims in the execution videos appear so calm. "They repeat the thing with them like 20 times. So when the real one comes, the prisoner will think it's just another mock execution," he said.

Surviving The Caliphate - Or Not

In Eski Mosul, a village on a bend in Iraq's Tigris River, Sheikh Abdullah Ibrahim lives in one of the larger houses, behind high walls with a garden. He looked exhausted as he showed AP journalists one IS vestige he's keeping: the death certificate for his wife, the group's black logo on top.

It's all he has left of her.

IS swept into the village of some 3,000 families in June last year, established its reign over a grim seven-month period, then fled in January when Kurdish fighters ran them out. IS forces remain dug in only a few miles away, so close that smoke can be seen from fighting on the front lines.

Ibrahim's wife, Buthaina, had been an outspoken human rights advocate and had run for the provincial council in Mosul. So when IS took over, fighters demanded she apply for a repentance card. "She said she'd never stoop so low," her husband said.

He knew the danger. He had seen the bodies of a dozen policemen in the street, shot in the head. He'd seen others thrown off buildings. He had heard talk of the dreaded "Khasfa," a deep natural sinkhole in the desert south of Mosul where the extremists boast of throwing bodies - or sometimes living victims.

Sheikh Abdullah Ibrahim poses with his son while holding an Islamic State group-issued death certificate - all that he has left of his wife, Buthaina Ibrahim, May 17, 2015. (AP Photo/Bram Janssen)

Ibrahim sent his wife away to safety for a few days, but she soon returned, missing their three daughters and two sons, he said. Her youngest was 2.

A few nights later, in early October, the militants came for her, he said.

Ibrahim and his wife were asleep, but their daughters were watching TV. "Wake up, dad, Daesh is in the front yard," they called out, using the group's Arabic acronym. Ibrahim saw the house was surrounded.

They demanded to see Buthaina. Ibrahim tried to protect her, he said, but she came out and confronted the IS extremists, demanding an explanation. An argument ensued, and one militant handcuffed the sheikh and knocked him across the head with a pistol. The men pushed Buthaina into their car, and took Ibrahim's as well.

A member of the powerful al-Jabour tribe, Ibrahim hoped his connections - and money - could win Buthaina's freedom.

He and fellow tribesmen went to the nearby town of Tal Afar, an IS stronghold from which many of the fighters who took Eski Mosul had come. There, he said, he met in a mosque with Abu Alaa al-Afari, a local IS commander who some Iraqi officials now believe has risen to become the No. 2 figure in the "caliphate."

Ibrahim begged for his wife's release, pointing out that she was still breastfeeding their youngest son, Arkam.

"It doesn't matter. Your children will become orphans," al-Afari replied, according to Ibrahim.

Another Eski Mosul resident, 31-year-old Fadi Mohammed, wishes that all he had gotten from IS was his brother's death certificate.

He and his brother, Mohammed, were both former policemen who had given up their weapons and signed repentance papers. But his brother was arrested after informants claimed he was part of an elite intelligence unit. Mohammed was sent to Mosul. In January, 13 days before the Kurds took back Eski Mosul, Mohammed said IS militants "brought us discs that showed his beheading."

Now, he said, "I want to blow myself up among Daesh. Even that won't satisfy me. If I chop them up, drink their blood and eat their hearts, it won't take away my pain."

Laying low was often key to survival in the "caliphate," several of those interviewed said. Best to stay home as much as possible, avoiding checkpoints of IS fighters and the "Hisba" committees, the dreaded enforcers of IS' innumerable regulations.

Armed members of the Hisba patrol the streets, cruising in SUVs with blackened windows and wearing Afghan-style baggy pants, long shirts and face masks, looking for behavior deemed unacceptable.

Members of the Islamic State group's vice police known as Hisba prepare to burn cigarettes and alcohol in Homs Province, Syria, May 3, 2015. (AP Photo/Militant Website)

Punishments for smoking, for wearing Western clothes or for playing the wrong radio station can vary from a fine to imprisonment for a few hours or days - often depending on the Hisba's mood. For more serious or repeat offenses, the fighters might bind the perpetrator to a pole in a town square for several days with his crime written on a sign around his neck.

Women try not to go out at all, most of those interviewed by AP said. If they do go to market, they sometimes avoid taking their husbands, sons or brothers with them: If they're harassed by the Hisba, their male relative might defend them and bring the Hisba's wrath.

It's not an unreasonable fear. Abu Zein, a 31-year-old who recently fled the eastern Syrian town of Muhassan, recounted how a Hisba member one day berated a woman for being improperly covered as she swept her porch. Her brother came out and argued, the fight escalated, the militant shot the brother, and the brother's relatives promptly killed the militant. Soon after, a larger contingent of Islamic State fighters descended on the house and killed eight members of the family, Abu Zein said.

Abu Zein said he was detained multiple times for various minor offenses, including visiting his uncle's grave.

During Islamic holidays late last year, he said, militants announced in mosques that it was forbidden to visit the graves of relatives, a holiday tradition that IS sees as encouraging polytheism. Abu Zein's uncle had died of cancer the year before, so he, his cousin and another relative decided to defy the ban.

As they approached the graveyard, IS fighters opened fire over their heads, shouting "Grave worshippers!" and "This is forbidden!" Abu Zein said he and his friends tried to reason with them. "You cannot stop me from visiting my father," cried Abu Zein's 20-year-old cousin - prompting one militant to slap him across the face. The three were arrested and detained for several hours before being released with a warning.

Sheikh Abdullah Ibrahim's wife, Buthaina, never reappeared after being taken by the militants.

Sheikh Mohammed Abdullah Ibrahim Aatiyah holds the death certificate of his wife Buthaina in Mosul, May 17, 2015. (AP Photo/Bram Janssen)

Shortly after her husband appealed for her release, he received the death certificate. A simple sheet of paper from an "Islamic court" with a judge's signature, it said only that Buthaina's death was verified, nothing more.

It is a horrifying document, but he's keeping it, he said, "because it has her name on it."

Escaping The Caliphate

Escape is not easy. Residents are banned from leaving their cities without first applying for permission, filling out a long form with all their personal details and setting property as a guarantee that IS will seize if they don't return. Women must apply to the Hisba to travel and are often refused permission, out of concern that they will not follow IS dress codes once they are out.

When Adnan's aunt needed cancer treatment, she applied to leave IS territory to get care. The IS refused but sent her to Mosul, paying for transport and some of the medical costs, though not her chemotherapy.

In March, after Adnan had spent 55 days in prison, a top IS leader in Raqqa freed about 40 inmates - including the young Syrian activist.

Adnan decided it was time for him to go. He paid a smuggler to drive him along dirt roads about 25 kilometers to the Tal Abyad border crossing, which at the time was in IS hands and was shut from the Turkish side, then paid another smuggler to get him into Turkey. "It was an adventure," he said, smiling.

Escape was much more harrowing for Ali, a 63-year-old appliance store owner from the Iraqi town of al-Zaab, near Mosul, who asked that his full name not be used to protect relatives still under IS rule. He told AP that when he decided to flee, he managed to convince local authorities he was only going on a three-day work trip. They gave him a permission slip without a guarantee of property, so he set out in his car with his wife, son and daughter-in-law.

Between them and freedom were three different checkpoints. At the first, fighters wrote down the model and license number of his car. At the second, they searched his car, then ordered him to return to the first checkpoint. There, the fighters told him his car registration was improper and he had no property guarantee.

"Your fate will be execution," he said they told him.

But in a show of how capricious life can be under the Islamic State, a commander at the checkpoint made a phone call and got approval to let Ali and his family pass. "God give him long life," Ali said of the commander. He said he'd rather have been killed right there at the checkpoint than be forced to drive back into IS-held al-Zaab.

In Eski Mosul, delivery from IS came to residents at the hands of Kurdish fighters. Amid the joy over liberation - and perhaps worry over being accused of having IS loyalties - many residents promptly discarded documents from the Islamic State.

Not Salim Ahmed. For nearly seven months, the 23-year-old former soldier had clung to his repentance card, always having it ready at checkpoints. He hated the card. He had refused to laminate it, unwilling to give it a sense of permanence.

Salim Ahmed, a former Iraqi Army member, holds the "repentance card" he received from the Islamic State group in June 2014 shortly after the militants took over his home village of Eski Mosul, May 27, 2015. (AP Photo/Bram Janssen)

Now IS is gone, but the fear instilled in him is not. He still carries his card.

"We live very close to their front line," he said. "One day, they might come back and ask me for my repentance card again."

SAVED BY CIGARETTES
Eski Mosul, Iraq, Sunday, June 21, 2015

It was a heart-racing moment. The cigarette smuggler was stuck in line at a checkpoint as, up ahead, Islamic State militants were searching cars. He was running a big risk: The militants have banned smoking and lighting up is punishable with a fine or broken finger. Selling cigarettes can be a death sentence.

Falah Abdullah Jamil, 30, relied on his quick wits and silver tongue.

When the fighters came to his vehicle at the checkpoint leading to his home village of Eski Mosul in northern Iraq, they asked what he had in his trunk.

"Nothing," he lied.

They popped open the trunk and found the 125 cartons of cigarettes he'd brought from Rabia, a town near the border with Syria.

"I swear, it's out of hunger," he said he pleaded with the men. The father of six told them he was the only breadwinner for his extended family and was helping his neighbors as well.

The fighters took him to the checkpoint commander, who warned Jamil he'd go to prison and his car would be confiscated. Jamil promised never to do it again. "Just let me go this time for the sake of my children," he said. "If I don't have money, what can I do? Should I steal? If I steal, you'll cut off my hand."

In an interview with The Associated Press in May, Jamil sat in his modest living room, describing how he survived nearly seven months of IS rule before the extremist group was run from town by Kurdish fighters.

The checkpoint commander ordered his subordinates out of the room, Jamil recalled. Once they were alone, he made his offer: "I will let you go if you give me cigarettes." Jamil asked him what brand. "Anything, just give me two cartons," the commander replied.

The commander "said he hadn't had a smoke for three days so when he saw the cigarettes, he was very happy," Jamil said with a laugh.

Iraqi civilians living under IS rule in Mosul, the group's biggest stronghold, told the AP that the militants actually control the cigarette black market, banning smoking in public while privately controlling the sale of cigarettes at an inflated price. They spoke anonymously for fear of retribution.

Falah Abdullah Jamil poses for a portrait in Eski Mosul. He was held as a prisoner by the Islamic State group for selling cigarettes - which are banned by the militants - and was tortured while in jail, May 18, 2015. (AP Photo/Bram Janssen)

Saad Eidou, 25, a displaced Iraqi from the town of Sinjar near the Syrian border, said that like everyone else, militants smoke in private. The cigarettes come in through Syria, where movement in and out of Turkey and non-IS areas is easier.

"They brought in cigarettes from Syria, where you probably won't pay more than 250 dinars ($0.20) for a pack, but they were selling it here for 1,000 dinars ($0.80)," said Bilal Abdullah, another resident of Eski Mosul. With IS gone, he took deep draws from a cigarette in public as he spoke.

In another incident, Jamil said, he was accused of selling cigarettes by a member of the Hisba, the vice patrol that ruthlessly enforces the group's regulations. Jamil denied it profusely: "I told him, yes, I used to, but I stopped selling. I told him no one sells anymore since you have forbidden it."

The Hisba official asked if any cigarettes were in Jamil's house. Jamil said no.

"He said, 'I will go and inspect your house, and if I find one pack of cigarettes I will execute you.'"

Jamil's bluff had just gotten more dangerous. He had 1,600 cartons of cigarettes hidden at home, he said with a wicked smile.

But he stuck by his story. "I told him, 'Go ahead, I haven't got anything.'"

Apparently convinced, the Hisba official had him sign a document vowing to never sell cigarettes or risk execution.

"I signed it - but I sold again. I didn't stop," Jamil said. "We had no flour, no rice, no food. I have children, and it was winter and was cold and there was no oil, no gas. ... We were living a hellish tragedy."

Chapter 2

INSIDE THE CALIPHATE

An Islamic State militant, center, distributes plastic bags full of stationery and other gifts to young Iraqi students at a school classroom in Mosul, northern Iraq, January 11, 2015. (AP Photo/Militant Website)

CARROT AND STICK
Beirut, Lebanon, Thursday, November 27, 2014

The Islamic State group is employing multiple tactics to subdue the Sunni Muslim tribes in Syria and Iraq under its rule, wooing some with gifts - everything from cars to feed for their animals - while brutally suppressing those that resist with mass killings.

The result is that the extremists face little immediate threat of an uprising by the tribes, which are traditionally the most powerful social institution in the large areas of eastern Syria and northern and western Iraq controlled by the group. Any U.S. drive to try to turn tribesmen against the militants, as the Americans did with Sunnis during the Iraq war, faces an uphill battle.

Some tribes in Syria and Iraq already oppose the Islamic State group. For example, the Shammar tribe, which spans the countries' border, has fought alongside Kurdish forces against the extremists in Iraq. The U.S. and Iraqi governments have proposed creating a national guard program that would arm and pay tribesmen to fight, though the effort has yet to get off the ground.

But in Syria in particular, tribes have no outside patron to bankroll or arm them to take on IS, leaving them with few options other than to bend to Islamic State domination or flee.

"There are people who want to go back and fight them," said Hassan Hassan, an analyst with the Delma Institute in Abu Dhabi. "But the circumstances now mean that you can't provoke ISIS because the strategy they've followed and tactics are to prevent any revolt from inside."

A mass grave for al-Jabouri tribesmen, who were killed in battles against Islamic States militants, in the town of Duluiyah, 45 miles north of Baghdad. Al-Jabouri Sunnis allied with Iraqi troops and Shiite militiamen took back the town from the Islamic State group in December. Sunni tribes that have stood up to the IS group have paid a heavy price, and anger at the Shiite-led government runs deep in the areas of northern and western Iraq that now make up the extremist group's self-styled caliphate, March 25, 2015. (AP Photo/Karim Kadim)

The rulers of the self-styled caliphate have mastered techniques of divide and rule. Tribes are powerful institutions that command the loyalty of their members across the largely desert regions of Syria and Iraq. But they are also far from cohesive. Large tribes are divided up into smaller sub-tribes and clans that can be pitted against each other. Such divisions also emerge on their own, often in connection to control over local resources like oil wells or land.

Also, the Islamic State group itself has roots in the tribes. Though hundreds of foreign fighters have flocked to join the group, most of its leaders and foot soldiers are Iraqis and Syrians - and often belong to tribes.

In eastern Syria's Deir el-Zour province, for example, the Ogeidat is one of the largest tribes. One of its major clans, the Bu Jamel, has been a staunch opponent of the extremists. Another, the Bakir, long ago allied itself to the group.

IS operatives use threats or offers of money or fuel to win public pledges of loyalty from senior tribal sheikhs. The group has also wooed younger tribesmen with economic enticements and promises of positions within IS, undermining the traditional power structure of the tribe.

"They offer many sweeteners," said Abu Ali al-Badie, a tribal leader from the central city of Palmyra in Syria's Homs province. "They go to the tribes and say, 'Why are you fighting against Muslims? We'll give you weapons and cars and guns, and we'll fight together.'"

"They offer diesel and fuel. They bring barley and animal feed from Iraq," he said. "They build wells at their own expense for the tribes and they say, 'Others have neglected your needs.'"

In Syria, IS has won the acceptance of many tribesmen in Raqqa and Deir el-Zour provinces by ending chaos that reigned when the areas were controlled by a patchwork of rebel warlords. IS provides services including electricity, fuel, water and telephone lines, as well as flour for bakeries, said Haian Dukhan, a researcher at the University of St. Andrews Center for Syrian Studies.

"Things have started to become stable to a degree, and this is something that people were really desperate about," said Dukhan.

The group has "tribal affairs" officials to handle relations with the tribes, calibrating its style to local dynamics. Often they will allow loyal tribesmen to run their communities' services, said Hassan.

The group also has removed its own commanders who caused tension with tribes in their areas. The idea, Hassan said, is "to remove some of the toxins."

At the same time, the group sends a clear message to those who resist.

In August, IS militants shot and beheaded hundreds of members of the Shueitat tribe in eastern Syria. Activists reported death tolls ranging from 200 to 700. Photographs in the Islamic State's English-language "Dabiq" magazine showed black-clad fighters shooting prisoners said to be Shueitat, lined up on the sandy ground.

In Iraq, IS killed more than 200 men, women and children from the Al Bu Nimr tribe in Anbar province, apparently in revenge for the tribe's siding with security forces and, in the past, with American troops. It has also shot dead several men from the Al Bu Fahd tribe.

"Everyone is hiding or fled. They will chop us in pieces if they see us," said Sheikh Naim al-Gaoud, a leader in the Al Bu Nimr. "They want us to support them and to join their fight. In return, they say they will let us live in peace."

As a result, Dukhan says there's little chance for a revolt unless tribes are confident the extremists are losing.

"I think that for the time being, seeing a large-scale uprising against IS is just a fantasy."

PAID HONEYMOON
Beirut, Lebanon, Tuesday, May 26, 2015

The honeymoon was a brief moment for love, away from the front lines of Syria's war. In the capital of the Islamic State group's self-proclaimed "caliphate," Syrian fighter Abu Bilal al-Homsi was united with his Tunisian bride for the first time after months chatting online. They married, then passed the days dining on grilled meats in Raqqa's restaurants, strolling along the Euphrates River and eating ice cream.

It was all made possible by the marriage bonus he received from the Islamic State group: $1,500 for him and his wife to get started on a new home, a family - and a honeymoon.

"It has everything one would want for a wedding," al-Homsi said of Raqqa - a riverside provincial capital that in the 18 months since IS took control has seen militants beheading opponents and stoning alleged adulteresses in public. Gunmen at checkpoints scrutinize passers-by for signs of anything they see as a violation of

Shariah, or Islamic law, as slight as a hint of hair gel. In the homes of some of the IS commanders in the city are women and girls from the Yazidi religious sect, abducted in Iraq and now kept as sex slaves.

Yazidi Kurds protest against the Islamic State group's invasion on Sinjar city one year ago, in Dohuk, northern Iraq. Thousands of Yazidi Kurdish women and girls have been sold into sexual slavery and forced to marry Islamic State militants, according to Human Rights organizations, Yazidi activists and observers, August 3, 2015. (AP Photo/Seivan M. Salim)

The Islamic State group is notorious for the atrocities it committed as it overran much of Syria and neighboring Iraq. But to its supporters, it is engaged in an ambitious project: building a new nation ruled by what radicals see as "God's law," made up of Muslims from around the world whose old nationalities have been erased and who have been united in the "caliphate."

To do that, the group has set up a generous welfare system to help settle and create lives for the thousands of jihadis - men and women - who have flocked to IS territory from the Arab world, Europe, Central Asia and the United States.

"It is not just fighting," said al-Homsi, who uses a nom de guerre. "There are institutions. There are civilians (that IS) is in charge of, and wide territories . It must help the immigrants marry.

These are the components of a state and it must look after its subjects." Al-Homsi spoke in a series of interviews with The Associated Press by Skype, giving a rare look into the personal life of an IS jihadi.

The new IS elite is visible in Raqqa, the biggest city in Syria under the extremists' rule.

Luxury houses and apartments, which once belonged to officials from the government of Syrian President Bashar Assad, have been taken over by the new IS ruling class, according to a member of an anti-IS media collective in the city who goes by the name of Abu Ibrahim al-Raqqawi.

Raqqa, at the center of IS-controlled territory, is cushioned from the fighting around its edges. Its supermarkets are well stocked and it boasts several internet cafes.

"The city is stable, has all the services and all that is needed. It is not like rural areas the group controls," al-Raqqawi said. "Raqqa is now the new New York" of the caliphate. Like others in his media collective, he uses a nickname for his security and doesn't specify his whereabouts.

Helping fighters marry is a key priority. Aside from the normal stipend, foreign fighters receive $500 when they marry to help them start a family. The 28-year-old al-Homsi got a particularly large bonus because his new wife is a doctor and speaks four languages.

The AP has spoken with al-Homsi repeatedly over the past three years, since he started as an activist covering the fighting in his home city of Homs in central Syria. An IT specialist before the civil war in 2011, al-Homsi always espoused ultraconservative views in media interviews, sympathizing with the idea of a caliphate.

He said he had supported IS as early as 2013. But it was in mid-2014, after a two-year punishing siege of Homs, that he turned into a fighter. When the siege ended in a May 2014 truce, al-Homsi emerged as an official IS member.

It was from his social media activity that he met his wife, who admired his online media briefings.

After communicating online, al-Homsi found out that her brother had joined the group and was in the eastern Syrian city of Deir al-Zour. As is customary, he went to ask her brother for her hand in marriage.

The 24-year-old bride-to-be traveled through Algeria to Turkey, and from there to Raqqa with a group of other women joining IS. They were housed in a guesthouse for women, where the IS women police force also resides.

Al-Homsi made the hazardous 150-mile (250-kilometer) journey from Homs to Raqqa to join her, after getting a recommendation from his local commanders.

It was a rare marriage of a Syrian male fighter with a foreign migrant. Usually, foreign women marry foreign fighters in IS.

During the few days of their honeymoon, al-Homsi and his bride enjoyed Raqqa's relative tranquility, riverside promenades and restaurants.

Then the couple travelled back to the Homs area, where IS fighters are holding ground against Assad's forces and rival rebel groups.

There, al-Homsi used the money from his grant to prepare a home for his new bride, and four kittens. The couple is now expecting a new baby and hoping for another cash injection, as the group can pay up to $400 as a bonus for each child.

For now the group provides a stipend of $50 a month for him and a similar amount for his wife.

He also has an allowance for his uniform and clothes, some household cleaning supplies, and a monthly food basket worth $65.

Soon after speaking to the AP, al-Homsi was back on the battlefield, among the fighters who took over the ancient city of Palmyra earlier this month.

"The fighter is on the front," al-Homsi said. "How will he bring food to the house?"

WATER AS A WEAPON
Baghdad, Iraq, Thursday, June 4, 2015

Islamic State militants have reduced the amount of water flowing to government-held areas in Iraq's western Anbar province, officials said, a move that highlights the use of water as a weapon of war and puts more pressure on Iraqi forces struggling to claw back ground held by the extremists in the Sunni heartland.

View of the dam in Mosul 225 miles northwest of Baghdad, October 31, 2007. (AP Photo/ Khalid Mohammed)

The development is not the first time that water has been used as a weapon in Mideast conflicts and in Iraq in particular. Earlier this year, the Islamic State group reduced the flow through a lock outside the militant-held town of Fallujah, also in Anbar province. But the extremists soon reopened it after criticism from residents.

Last summer, IS militants took control of the Mosul Dam - the largest in Iraq - and threatened to flood Baghdad and other major cities, but Iraqi and Kurdish forces, backed by U.S. airstrikes, later recaptured the facility.

The battle for the dam followed the Islamic State's blitz across much of western and northern Iraq earlier last year, an advance that captured key Anbar cities and also Mosul, Iraq's second-largest city that lies to the north of Baghdad. The Islamic State group also gained large swaths of land in neighboring Syria and proclaimed a self-styled caliphate on the territory it controls, imposing its harsh interpretation of Islamic law, or Sharia.

Last month, the IS captured Ramadi, the provincial capital of Anbar, marking its most significant victory since a U.S.-led coalition began an air campaign against the extremists last August.

On Wednesday, IS militants closed the locks on a militant-held dam on the Euphrates River near Ramadi, reducing the flow downstream and threatening irrigation systems and water treatment plants in nearby areas controlled by troops and tribes opposed to the extremist group.

Anbar councilman Taha Abdul-Ghani said the move will not only make the lives of people living in the affected areas more difficult but it could also pose a threat to the security forces fighting to recapture Ramadi. If water levels drop significantly, he said, the extremists could cross the Euphrates River on foot.

"The militants might take advantage of that and attack troops deployed along the river" and the nearby Habaniya military base, Abdul-Ghani told The Associated Press.

The base has been used as a staging ground for Iraqi troops and allied Shiite militias in the fight against the militants in Ramadi and surrounding areas.

Thousands of people in government-held towns of Khalidiya and Habaniya are already suffering from shortages of drinking water because purification plants along the Euphrates have all but shut down because of already low water levels on account of the summer weather. The residents of the towns get only two hours a day of water through their pipes, he said.

"With the summer heat and lack of water, the lives of these people are in danger and some are thinking of leaving their homes," added Abdul-Ghani, and urged the government to use the air force to bomb some of the gates of al-Warar dam and release the water.

He said there was no impact on Shiite areas in central and southern Iraq, saying water is being diverted to those areas from the Tigris River.

Abu Ahmed, a farmer with a vegetable farm near Khalidiya, said he could lose all his crops because of lack of irrigation water. Now, the water is lower than level of his water pumping machines.

"I used to irrigate my crops every three day. If the situation continues like this, my vegetables will die," said Abu Ahmed, using his nickname because of fears for his own life.

The United Nations said Wednesday it was looking into reports that IS had reduced the flow of water through the al-Warar dam.

"The use of water as a tool of war is to be condemned in no uncertain terms," the spokesman for the U.N. secretary-general, Stephane Dujarric, told reporters. "These kinds of reports are disturbing, to say the least."

He said the U.N. and humanitarian partners will try to "fill in the gaps" to meet water needs for the affected population.

On Thursday, U.N. officials meeting in Brussels to launch an Iraqi aide operation urgently called for $497 million in donations to provide shelter, food, water and other life-saving services for the next six months to Iraqis displaced or affected by the fighting between government forces and the Islamic State group.

The needs of Iraqis affected by the fighting are huge and growing, the officials said, with more than 8 million people requiring immediate support, and potentially 10 million by the end of 2015.

Lise Grande, the U.N.'s humanitarian coordinator for Iraq, said the aid operation, which she called one of the most complex and volatile in the world, was hanging by a thread.

"Humanitarian partners have been doing everything they can to help. But more than 50 per cent of the operation will be shut down or cut back if money is not received immediately," Grande told members of the European Parliament, according to a U.N. news release. The consequences of such a reduction in aid, Grande said, would be "catastrophic."

"While we search for solutions to end the violence, we must do everything in our power to help," said U.N. Assistant Secretary-General for Humanitarian Affairs Kyung-Wha Kang, also in Brussels. "The people of Iraq need our help, now."

Earlier this week, Iraqi Prime Minister Haider al-Abadi had pressed his case at a Paris conference, calling for more support from the 25 countries in the U.S.-led coalition fighting the militant group, asking for more armament and ammunition.

"We're relying on ourselves, but fighting is very hard this way," al-Abadi said before the conference Tuesday.

The coalition has mustered a mix of airstrikes, intelligence sharing and assistance for Iraqi ground operations against the extremists. Al-Abadi said more was needed, with Iraq reeling after troops pulled out of Ramadi without a fight and abandoned U.S.-supplied tanks and weapons.

TWO FACES OF THE ISLAMIC STATE
Beirut, Lebanon, Friday, July 10, 2015

During the Muslim holy month of Ramadan, the Islamic State group is showing two faces to the millions who live under its rule in

Iraq and Syria - handing out food and alms to the poor to tout their adherence to the month's spirit of compassion while meting out sharp punishment to anyone caught breaking the daily fast.

The double approach reflects the policy that the extremist group has followed ever since it overran large parts of the two countries and declared a "caliphate" in its territory last year. It has sought to build public support by providing services and acting as a functioning government, even as it imposes its strict version of Islamic law through violence.

In the Iraqi city of Mosul, the biggest city under IS rule, those who break the fast can be punished by being put in a cage in a public square for hours or for several days, said one resident, speaking on condition he be identified only by his first name, Omar, for his own security. In parts of Syria, violators are tied to a wooden cross in public, according to the Syrian Observatory for Human Rights, which monitors the situation in the country. Other residents and activists reported fast-violators being flogged.

Rami Abdurrahman, gestures during an interview with The Associated Press in Coventry, England. The 42-year-old operates the Syrian Observatory for Human Rights from his house in the cathedral city of Coventry — and a review of recent media coverage suggests its running tally of killings and clashes is the most frequently cited individual source of information on Syria's civil war for the world's leading news organizations, October 10, 2013. (AP Photo/Raphael Satter)

Ramadan, which began in mid-June and ends next week, is a time when Muslims around the world seek to be closer to God, refraining from food, water, smoking and sex from dawn to sunset, offering extra prayers, reading the Quran, showing charity for the poor and cementing friendships and family ties. Usually, it's festive after sunset, with families out visiting each other or gathering at street cafes, playing backgammon, cards or smoking waterpipes.

In the IS-ruled city of Fallujah in western Iraq, residents have been told by the group's authorities not to gather at coffee shops - and anyway, smoking and games are banned. IS has also ordered men to observe a modest dress code during Ramadan, meaning no sleeveless shirts or shorts, common attire for Iraqi men to cope with the unforgiving summer heat.

"We've lost the beautiful Ramadan atmosphere we are accustomed to," said Mohammed Ahmed Jassim, a 52-year old grocer and father of three in Fallujah.

"Before, you could tell it is Ramadan in every corner in the city," he said. "Now everyone is staying put at home waiting for his fate."

Many under IS rule are also enduring higher food prices, particularly for produce and bread, in part because of fighting near the Turkish border that saw farmlands burned and because of the takeover by Kurdish fighters last month of Syria's Tal Abyad border crossing, formerly a key supply route for IS.

At the same time, the extremists have unleashed some of their most horrifying brutalities during Ramadan. In the first week of the month, the group released a video purporting to show the killing of 16 men it described as spies by drowning them in a cage lowered to the bottom of a pool, decapitating them with explosives or firing a rocket-propelled grenade at a car they were forced into.

Last week, it posted a video that purports to show the killings of some two dozen Syrian army soldiers by young IS fighters with a bullet to the head inside the ruins of the ancient town of Palmyra, with an audience of several hundred people.

An IS call for jihad during Ramadan appears to have triggered deadly attacks in Tunisia, Kuwait, Egypt and France over the past weeks. In Syria, IS fighters infiltrated the border town of Kobani, battling Kurdish forces for two days and killing some 250 civilians, including as many as 100 children, many in their homes, according to activists.

A hooded Tunisian police officer stands guard ahead of the visit of top security officials of Britain, France, Germany and Belgium at the scene of Friday's shooting attack in front of the Imperial Marhaba hotel in the Mediterranean resort of Sousse, Tunisia, June 29, 2015. (AP Photo/Abdeljalil Bounhar)

The Islamic State group's powerful media machine has also been using Ramadan to promote itself. One carefully choreographed online video depicted what was said to be the life of its fighters on the frontline during the fast, showing them firing on enemies supposedly over the horizon, and then later sitting down for a meal of rice, chicken, dates, pickles and bread to break the fast at sunset.

The group also regularly posts online photos of its Ramadan charity. Activists in Iraq and Syria say the militants distribute Ramadan food baskets that include rice, crushed wheat, sugar and cooking oil. They also make dates, juice and mineral water available in mosques for those praying when the day's fast ends.

In Fallujah, IS militants slaughtered sheep and cows and distributed their meat to residents on the first day of Ramadan, according to residents there.

Occasionally, IS authorities organize a free "Iftar," the sunset meal, in public squares or in mosques, according to Bari Abdul-Latif, an activist from the IS-held Syrian town of al-Bab in Aleppo province. They also sell cylinders of cooking gas at one-fifth of the market price during Ramadan.

"They are planting the idea in people's minds that they are in control," said Abdul-Latif.

Chapter 3

BEHEAD THE DOLL

Yahya, a 14-year-old from the Yazidi religious minority, talks about life in an Islamic State training camp, during an interview from a camp for internally displaced people outside Dohuk in the northern Kurdish region of Iraq. He explained how more than 120 children inside the camp had to line up and they were each given a doll and a sword, waiting for their next lesson by their Islamic State group instructors: Behead the doll, July 12, 2015. (AP Photo/Bram Janssen)

FIGHT TO THE DEATH
Baghdad, Iraq, Wednesday, July 8, 2015

Bearded and wearing bright blue bandanas, the Islamic State group's "special forces" unit gathered around their commander just before they attacked the central Syrian town of al-Sukhna. "Victory or martyrdom," they screamed, pledging their allegiance to God and vowing never to retreat.

The IS calls them "Inghemasiyoun," Arabic for "those who immerse themselves." The elite shock troops are possibly the deadliest weapon in the extremist group's arsenal: Fanatical and disciplined, they infiltrate their targets, unleash mayhem and fight to the death, wearing explosives belts to blow themselves up among their opponents if they face defeat. They are credited with many of the group's stunning battlefield successes - including the capture of al-Sukhna in May after the scene shown in an online video released by the group.

"They cause chaos and then their main ground offensive begins," said Redur Khalil, spokesman of the U.S.-backed Kurdish People's Protection Units, which have taken the lead in a string of military successes against the IS in Syria.

Kurdish fighters with the Kurdish People's Protection Units, or YPG, wave their yellow triangular flag in the outskirts of Tal Abyad, Syria, June 15, 2015. (AP Photo/Lefteris Pitarakis)

Though best known for its horrific brutalities - from its grotesque killings of captives to enslavement of women - the Islamic State group has proved to be a highly organized and flexible fighting force, according to senior Iraqi military and intelligence officials and Syrian Kurdish commanders on the front lines.

Its tactics are often creative, whether it's using a sandstorm as cover for an assault or a lone sniper tying himself to the top of a palm tree to pick off troops below. Its forces nimbly move between conventional and guerrilla warfare, using the latter to wear down their opponents before massed fighters backed by armored vehicles, Humvees and sometimes even artillery move to take over territory. The fighters incorporate suicide bombings as a fearsome battlefield tactic to break through lines and demoralize enemies, and they are constantly honing them to make them more effective. Recently, they beefed up the front armor of the vehicles used in those attacks to prevent gunfire from killing the driver or detonating explosives prematurely.

Those strategies are being carried over into new fronts, appearing in Egypt in last week's dramatic attack by an IS-linked militant group against the military in the Sinai Peninsula.

Religious flags, photographs and tributes to 21 victims of a suicide bombing, claimed by the Islamic State group, of a Shiite mosque are seen attached to their graves at a cemetery in Qudeeh, Saudi Arabia. The Islamic State group is extending its reach in Saudi Arabia, expanding the scope of its attacks and drawing in new recruits with its radical ideology, May 30, 2015. (AP Photo/Hasan Jamali)

Andreas Krieg, a professor at King's College London who embedded with Iraqi Kurdish fighters last fall, said IS local commanders are given leeway to operate as they see fit. They "have overall orders on strategy and are expected to come up with the most efficient ways of adapting it," he said. The group "is very much success oriented, results oriented." That's a strong contrast to the rigid, inefficient and corrupt hierarchies of the Iraqi and Syrian militaries, where officers often fear taking any action without direct approval from higher up.

IS fighters are highly disciplined - swift execution is the punishment for deserting battle or falling asleep on guard duty, Iraqi officers said. The group is also flush with weaponry looted from Iraqi forces that fled its blitzkrieg a year ago, when IS overtook the northern city of Mosul and other areas. Much of the heavy weapons it holds - including artillery and tanks - have hardly been used, apparently on reserve for a future battle.

An Iraqi soldier picks up items on display with weapons and ammunition confiscated after security forces regained control of the towns of al-Karma and Saqlawiyah near Fallujah, at al-Taji Camp north of Baghdad, Iraq, July 10, 2015. (AP Photo/Karim Kadim)

Iraqi army Lieutenant General Abdul-Wahab al-Saadi said IS stands out in its ability to conduct multiple battles simultaneously.

"In the Iraqi army, we can only run one big battle at a time," said al-Saadi, who was wounded twice in the past year as he led forces that retook the key cities of Beiji and Tikrit from IS.

Even the group's atrocities are in part a tactic, aimed at terrorizing its enemies and depicting itself as an unstoppable juggernaut. In June 2014, the group boasted of killing hundreds of Shiites in Iraq's security forces, issuing photos of the massacre. It regularly beheads captured soldiers, releasing videos of the killings online. It is increasing the shock value: Recent videos showed it lowering captives in a cage into a pool to drown and blowing off the heads of others with explosive wire around their necks.

The number of IS fighters in Iraq and Syria is estimated between 30,000 to 60,000, according to the Iraqi officers. Former army officers of ousted Iraqi dictator Saddam Hussein have helped the group organize its fighters, a diverse mix from Europe, the United States and Arab and Central Asian nations. Veteran jihadis with combat experience in Afghanistan, Chechnya or Somalia have also brought valuable experience, both in planning and as role models to younger fighters.

"They tend to use their foreign fighters as suicide bombers," said Patrick Skinner, a former CIA officer who now directs special operations for The Soufan Group, a private geopolitical risk assessment company. "People go to the Islamic State looking to die, and the Islamic State is happy to help them."

The group's tactics carried it to an overwhelming sweep of northern and western Iraq a year ago, capturing Mosul, Iraq's second-biggest city. Shortly thereafter, IS leader Abu Bakr al-Baghdadi declared a "caliphate" spanning its territory in Iraq and Syria.

In May, it captured Ramadi, capital of Iraq's vast western Anbar province, in a humiliation for Iraqi forces. In Syria, it seized the central city of Palmyra.

The elite shock troops were crucial in the capture of Ramadi. First came a wave of more than a dozen suicide bombings that hammered the military's positions in the city, then the fighters moved in during a sandstorm. Iraqi troops crumbled and fled as a larger IS force marched in.

"The way they took Ramadi will be studied for a while," Skinner said. "They have the ability to jump back and forth between traditional (military operations) and terrorism." He said a similar combination of suicide bombings ahead of ground forces was used in last week's Sinai attacks in Egypt.

Since US-led airstrikes in Syria and Iraq have made it more difficult for the group's forces to advance, IS has lost ground. Iraqi troops and Shiite militiamen retook areas to the south and northeast of Baghdad, the oil refinery city of Beiji and Saddam Hussein's hometown of Tikrit north of the capital.

In Syria, Kurdish fighters backed by heavy U.S. airstrikes wrested the border town of Kobani from the IS after weeks of devastating battles. More recently, IS lost Tal Abyad, another Syrian town on the Turkish border.

Despite that loss, IS shock troops attacked Kobani last month. Around 70 of them infiltrated and battled a much larger Kurdish force for two days, apparently on a mission not to retake the town but to cause chaos.

They were all slain, but not before killing more than 250 civilians, including roughly 100 children, and more than 30 Kurdish fighters. At the same time, they attacked the northeast Syrian city of Hassakeh, driving out thousands of people and still holding out in parts of the city despite continued fighting. Last week, they carried out a bloody incursion into Tal Abyad, again fighting until they were all killed but demonstrating their relentlessness.

Islamic State militants fire an anti-tank missile in Hassakeh, northeast Syria, June 26, 2015. (AP Photo/Militant Website)

"We are still nursing our wounds in Kobani," said Ghalia Nehme, a Syrian Kurdish commander who fought in last month's battle. "From what we saw, they weren't planning to leave alive. It seems they were longing for heaven," she said.

The use of suicide bombings has forced IS's opponents to adapt. Al-Saadi defied his own Iraqi military commanders who demanded a fast assault to retake Beiji. Instead, he adopted a slow, methodical march from a base near Tikrit, moving only a few miles each day while clearing roads of explosives and setting up barriers against suicide attacks. It took him three weeks to go 25 miles to Beiji, fighting the whole way and fending off more than two dozen suicide attacks, then another week to take Beiji, but he succeeded with minimal casualties.

IS also has adapted, and recently began using remote controlled aircraft fitted with cameras to film enemy positions. It is believed to have agents within the military. It also has superior communications equipment, using two-way radios with a longer range than the Iraqi military's, said Major General Ali Omran, commander of Iraq's 5th Division.

Omran said that when the extremists figured out the military was listening in on its radio frequencies, it switched to more secure lines but continued using the infiltrated frequencies to feed the military false information.

Even IS supply chains are robust. Its fighters' rations often include grilled meat kebabs and chicken, better than what Iraqi troops eat, Omran said.

But IS has its vulnerabilities, noted Skinner. It has no air force. And its open, state-like organization gives an opportunity for spies to infiltrate, something the group clearly fears given the many killings of people it suspects of espionage. It also faces internal strains, trying to control and direct its multi-national personnel.

"We think of them as this spooky faceless organization that runs seamlessly," Skinner said. "I imagine it's probably the hardest organization to run, because it's staffed with unstable, violent people."

BEHEAD THE DOLL
Sanliurfa, Turkey, Monday, July 20, 2015

The children each received a doll and a sword. Then they were lined up, more than 120 of them, and given their next lesson by their Islamic State group instructors: Behead the doll.

A 14-year-old who was among the line of abducted boys from Iraq's Yazidi religious minority said that at first, he couldn't cut it right - he chopped once, twice, three times.

"Then they taught me how to hold the sword, and they told me how to hit. They told me it was the head of the infidels," the boy, renamed Yahya by his Islamic State captors, recalled in an interview last week with The Associated Press in northern Iraq, where he fled after escaping the IS training camp.

When Islamic State extremists overran Yazidi towns and villages in northern Iraq last year, they butchered older men. Many of the women and girls they captured were given to IS loyalists as sex slaves. But dozens of young Yazidi boys like Yahya had a different fate: the group sought to re-educate them. They forced them to convert to Islam from their ancient faith and then tried to turn them into jihadi extremist fighters.

It is part of a concerted effort by the extremists to build a new generation of militants, according to a series of AP interviews with residents who fled or still live under IS in Syria and Iraq. The group is recruiting teens and children, using cash, gifts, intimidation and brainwashing. As a result, children have been plunged into the group's atrocities. Young boys have been turned into killers, shooting captives in the head in videos issued by the group. Last week, for the first time, a video showed a child involved in a beheading: a boy who appeared younger than 13 decapitating a Syrian army captain. Kids also have been used as suicide bombers.

Abu Hafs Naqshabandi, a Syrian sheikh who runs a center for Islamic religious studies meant to counter the Islamic State group indoctrination, speaks during an interview with the Associated Press, near the Turkish-Syrian border city of Sanliurfa, southern Turkey. In refugee camps, on streets and in mosques, children have become prime targets for the Islamic State group's outreach and propaganda. Using various methods, including cash rewards, intimidation and brainwashing, IS fighters have made children and teens a focus of their recruitment efforts, running schools, orphanages and training camps, April 19, 2015. (AP Photo/Hussein Malla)

In schools and mosques, the militants infuse children with their extremist doctrine, often turning them against their own parents. Fighters in the street befriend children with toys. IS training camps for children churn out the Ashbal, Arabic for "lion cubs," young fighters for the "caliphate" that IS has declared across the regions it controls. A caliphate is a historic form of Islamic rule that the group claims to be reviving, though the vast majority of Muslims reject its claim.

"They are planting extremism and terrorism in young people's minds," said Abu Hafs Naqshabandi, a Syrian sheikh in the Turkish city of Sanliurfa, where he runs religion classes for refugees to counter IS ideology. "I am terribly worried about future generations."

The indoctrination mainly targets the Sunni Muslim children living under IS rule. But the abduction of the Yazidis, whom IS considers heretics ripe for slaughter, shows how the group sought even to take another community's youth, erase its past and replace it with IS radicalism.

Syrian boy Ahmad, 7, whose parents went missing in Syria, attends a class of religious lessons at an Islamic teaching center designed to counter Islamic State group indoctrination, near the Turkish-Syrian border city of Sanliurfa, southern Turkey, April 19, 2015. (AP Photo/Hussein Malla)

The camp where Yahya and other Yazidi boys were taken was the Farouq Institute for Cubs in the Syrian city of Raqqa, which serves as the extremists' de facto capital. The boys were given Muslim Arabic names to replace their Kurdish-language names. Yahya asked that the AP not use his real name because of fears of retaliation against himself or his family.

Yahya, his little brother, their mother and hundreds of Yazidis were captured when the extremists overran the town of Sulagh in northern Iraq last year. They were taken to Syria, where the brothers were separated from their mother and put in the Farouq camp, along with other Yazidi boys aged between 8 and 15, Yahya told the AP.

He spent nearly five months there, undergoing eight to 10 hours a day of training, including running, exercising, weapons' training and studying the Quran. The boys hit each other in some exercises. Yahya said he punched his 10-year-old brother, knocking out his tooth.

"I was forced to do that. (The trainer) said that if I didn't do it, he'd shoot me," he said. "They ... told us it would make us tougher. They beat us everywhere with their fists."

In an online IS video of the Farouq camp, boys in camouflage do calisthenics. Some repeat back religious interpretation texts they have memorized justifying the killing of prisoners and infidels. An IS fighter sitting with a line of boys says they have studied the principles of jihad "so that in the coming days God Almighty can put them in the front lines to battle the infidels."

IS videos from other training camps show young boys in military fatigues marching with weapons, crawling under barbed wire and practicing shooting. One child lies on the ground and fires a machine gun; he's so small that the recoil bounces his whole body back a few inches. Other scenes show boys undergoing endurance training. They stand unmoving as a trainer punches them or hits their heads with a pole. They lie on the ground as a trainer walks on them.

Most of the children look stony-faced, their only emotion a momentary flicker as they try to remember texts they are told to recite.

"By God, (Barack) Obama and all those allied against the State, we will kill you. Who will? We lion cubs of the caliphate," proclaims one boy who looks younger than 10, holding an automatic rifle as he addresses the U.S. president.

IS has claimed to have hundreds of such camps, though the true number is not known - nor the number of children who have gone through the training. The Syrian Observatory for Human Rights, a Britain-based organization that follows the Syrian war, said it documented at least 1,100 Syrian children under 16 who joined IS so far this year, many of whom were then sent to fight in Syria and Iraq. At least 52 were killed, including eight who blew themselves up in suicide attacks, the organization said.

The effects of the indoctrination are chilling. In an IS video released last month, 25 young boys with pistols take position between 25 captured Syrian soldiers brought into the ancient Roman amphitheater in the Syrian city of Palmyra. Unflinching, each boy shoots a soldier in the back of the head. Previous videos have shown boys killing what IS alleged were an Israeli spy and two Russian agents.

Often, recruiting starts on the streets of IS-held areas at outdoor booths called "media points," where militants show young people propaganda videos. Militants hold outdoor events for children, distributing soft drinks, candy and biscuits, along with religious pamphlets and CDs. Bit by bit, the idea of jihad as a duty is drilled into young minds. The Islamic State group's acolytes distribute toys in the street and tell children to call them if they want to join, according to an anti-IS activist who recently fled Raqqa.

"They tell (adults) ... 'We have given up on you, we care about the new generation,'" the activist said, speaking on condition of anonymity to preserve the safety of relatives living under IS rule.

One Raqqa resident told the AP of his neighbor's 16-year-old son, Ahmed, who spent long hours at his local IS-run mosque. Ahmed began picking fights with his family, telling his older brother and parents they were bad Muslims because they didn't pray.

In November, when he told his family he wanted to join IS, his mother wept, while his father told him his family would never take him back. The teen vanished 10 days later. His father was told by IS members that his son was fighting for the group in eastern Syria and he should be proud of him.

"They turned him against his family. They convinced him they were apostates," said the neighbor, a friend of the parents who also spoke on condition of anonymity for fear of retaliation. Ahmed's family members refused to speak to the AP, fearing IS might punish their son for anything they say.

Some parents in IS-run areas take their children out of schools to avoid IS brainwashing.

In Eski Mosul, a town in northern Iraq recently liberated from IS, residents showed the AP a book the militants used to lecture children titled "The Clear Evidence of the Heresy of Those Who Support the Crusader Campaign against the Islamic Caliphate."

"America is the head of the infidels, atheism and the central base of corruption and moral decay - it is the land of shame, crime, filth, and evil," the book says.

Umm Ali, a woman from the predominantly Kurdish Syrian town of Afrin who worked in fields held by the extremists in Aleppo province, said her sons were approached by Islamic State members several times, and she hated that children saw beheadings and other punishments carried out in public squares.

A girl holds a broom in the town of Eski Mosul, Iraq, which had been under the control of the Islamic State group for months. Most residents stayed in the town after it was liberated by Kurdish Peshmerga forces in January 2015, May 27, 2015. (AP Photo/Bram Janssen)

"I saw one man hanging from a pole, his body badly tortured. Children were taking photographs. It's horrible, horrible," she said, crying. She spoke at a health clinic in Gaziantep, Turkey, where she had fled with her six children.

Even in refugee camps, children are not out of IS reach. Often under the guise of humanitarian organizations, the IS organizes religious lessons to recruit people, said Naqshabandi, the Syrian sheik. The militants would pay students who enroll 300 Turkish liras ($110) a month, said Abu Omar, a field worker at the camps.

Life and Death in ISIS

"They taught us to hate," said a 15-year-old former refugee camp resident who witnessed IS indoctrination, speaking on condition of anonymity to protect himself and his family. "This is what they teach" - and he moved his hand sharply across his throat.

Yahya, the Yazidi boy, escaped the IS training camp in early March, when IS fighters left to carry out an attack. As the remaining guards slept, he said he and his brother slipped away, telling the other children he was going to throw out the garbage. He asked one friend to come with them, but the friend chose to stay. He was Muslim now, the friend said. He liked Islam.

Yahya knew his mother was staying in a house nearby with other abducted Yazidis, since he had occasionally been allowed to visit her. So he and his brother went to her, and then travelled to the IS-held northern Syrian city of Minbaj with some fellow Yazidis. There, they stayed with a Russian member of IS, Yahya said. After that, he contacted his uncle in northern Iraq, who negotiated to pay the Russian for the two boys and their mother. A deal struck, the Russian sent them to Turkey to meet the uncle and they made their way to the city of Dohuk in the Kurdish autonomous zone of northern Iraq.

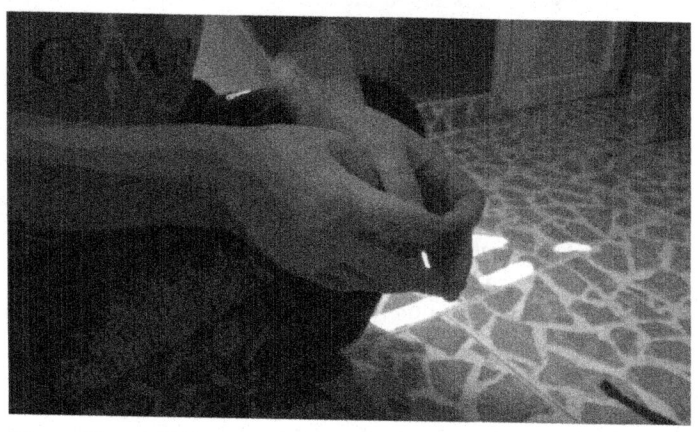

Yahya, a 14-year-old from the Yazidi minority, speaks to the Associated Press from a camp for the internally displaced outside Dohuk in the northern Kurdish region of Iraq about life in an Islamic State training camp. "They taught me how to hold the sword, and they told me how to hit. They told me it was the head of the infidels," he recalled how he was taught to chop off the head of a doll, July 12, 2015. (AP Photo/Bram Janssen)

Now in a house in Dohuk rented by the uncle, Yahya and his brother spend much of their time watching TV, grateful to be back with their mother and away from the terrifying camp, where they were forced to watch videos of beheadings.

"I was scared," Yahya said. "I knew I wouldn't be able to behead someone like that. Even as an adult."

SUMMER CAMP IN IRAQ
Baghdad, Iraq, Tuesday, July 28, 2015

In the steamy Baghdad night, sweat poured down the faces of the Iraqi teens as they marched around a school courtyard, training for battle against the Islamic State group.

This is summer camp in Iraq, set up by the country's largest paramilitary force after Iraq's top Shiite cleric issued an edict calling on students as young as middle-school age to use their summer vacations to prepare to fight the Sunni extremists.

These young fighters could have serious implications for the U.S.-led coalition, which provides billions of dollars in military and economic aid to the Iraqi government. The Child Soldiers Prevention Act of 2008 says the United States cannot provide certain forms of military support, including foreign military financing and direct commercial sales to governments that recruit and use child soldiers or support paramilitaries or militias that do.

Hundreds of students have gone through training at the dozens of such camps run by the Popular Mobilization Forces, the government-sanctioned umbrella group of mostly Shiite militias. It is impossible to say how many went on to fight IS, since those who do so go independently. But this summer, The Associated Press saw over a dozen armed boys on the front line in western Anbar province, including some as young as 10.

Of around 200 cadets in a training class visited by the AP this month, about half were under the age of 18, with some as young as 15. Several said they intended to join their fathers and older brothers on the front lines.

Dressed in military fatigues, 15-year-old Asam Riad was among dozens of youths doing high-knee marches at the school, his chest puffed out to try to appear as tall as the older cadets.

"We've been called to defend the nation," the scrawny boy asserted, his voice cracking as he vowed to join the PMF. "I am not scared because my brothers are fighting alongside me."

Another 15-year-old in the class, Jaafar Osama, said he used to want to be an engineer when he grows up, but now he wants to be a fighter. His father is a volunteer fighting alongside the Shiite militias in Anbar and his older brother is fighting in Beiji, north of Baghdad.

Iraqi volunteers with Popular Mobilization Forces train at a volunteers center in Baghdad. The Associated Press has found that militia forces battling the Islamic State group are actively training children under 18 years old, July 14, 2015. (AP Photo/Vivian Salama)

"God willing, when I complete my training I will join them, even if it means sacrificing my life to keep Iraq safe," he said.

It's yet another way minors are being dragged into Iraq's brutal war as the military, Shiite militias, Sunni tribes and Kurdish fighters battle to take back territory from Islamic State militants who seized much of the country's north and west last year. The Sunni extremists have aggressively enlisted children as young as 10 for combat, as suicide bombers and as executioners in their horrifying videos. This month, Human Rights Watch said that Syrian Kurdish militias fighting the militants continue to deploy underage fighters.

The U.S. does not work directly with the Popular Mobilization Forces and has distanced itself from the Iranian-backed militias which are among the fighters under its umbrella. But the PMF receives weapons and funding from the Iraqi government and is trained by the Iraqi military, which receives its training from the U.S.

When informed of the AP findings, the U.S. Embassy in Baghdad issued a statement saying the U.S. is "very concerned by the allegations on the use of child soldiers in Iraq among some Popular Mobilization forces in the fight against ISIL," using an acronym for the militant group. "We have strongly condemned this practice around the world and will continue to do so."

For Iraq's Shiite majority, the war against the Islamic State group - which views them as heretics to be killed - is a life-or-death fight for which the entire community has mobilized.

Last year, when IS took over the northern city of Mosul, stormed to the doorstep of Baghdad and threatened to destroy Shiite holy sites, Iraq's top Shiite cleric, Ayatollah Ali al-Sistani, called on the public to volunteer to fight. So great was his influence that hundreds of thousands of men came forward to join the hastily-established Popular Mobilization Forces along with some of the long-established Shiite militias, many of which receive support from Iran.

Then, on June 9, as schools let out, al-Sistani issued a new fatwa urging young people in college, high school and even middle school to use their summer vacations to "contribute to (the country's) preservation by training to take up arms and prepare to fend off risk if this is required."

In response, the Popular Mobilization Forces set up summer camps in predominantly Shiite neighborhoods from Baghdad to Basra. A spokesman for the group, Kareem al-Nouri, said the camps give "lessons in self-defense" and underage volunteers are expected to return to school by September, not go to the battle front.

A spokesman for the Iraqi prime minister's office echoed that. There may be "some isolated incidents" of underage fighters joining combat on their own, Saad al-Harithi told the AP. "But there has been no instruction by the Marjaiyah (the top Shiite religious authority) or the Popular Mobilization Forces for children to join the battle."

"We are a government that frowns upon children going to war," he said.

Iraqi volunteers with Popular Mobilization Forces train in Baghdad, July 14, 2015. (AP Photo/Vivian Salama)

But the line between combat training and actually joining combat is blurry, and it is weakly enforced by the Popular Mobilization Forces. Multiple militias operate under its umbrella, with fighters loyal to different leaders who often act independently.

At the training camp in a middle-class Shiite neighborhood of western Baghdad earlier this month, the young cadets spoke openly of joining battle in front of their trainers, who did nothing to contradict them.

Neighborhood youths spent their evenings in training every night during the holy month of Ramadan, which ended in mid-July, with mock exercises held every few days since then for those who wish to continue.

The boys ran through the streets practicing urban warfare techniques, since the toughest battles with the Islamic State group are likely to involve street fighting. They were taught to hold, control and aim light weapons, though they didn't fire them. They also took part in public service activities like holding blood drives and collecting food and clothing.

Earlier this summer, at one of the hottest front lines, near the IS-held city of Fallujah in western Anbar province, the AP spoke to a number of young boys, some heavily armed, among the Shiite militiamen.

Baghdad natives Hussein Ali, 12, and his cousin Ali Ahsan, 14, said they joined their fathers on the battlefield after they finished their final exams. Carrying AK-47's, they paced around the Anbar desert, boasting of their resolve to liberate the predominantly Sunni province from IS militants.

A young Shiite volunteer militiaman passes under the Quran, the Muslim holy book, as a Shiite cleric blesses him before going to the battlefield against Islamic State fighters. The Associated Press has found that militia forces battling the Islamic State group are actively training children under 18 years old, March 15, 2015. (AP Photo/Khalid Mohammed)

"It's our honor to serve our country," Hussein Ali said, adding that some of his schoolmates were also fighting. When asked if he was afraid, he smiled and said no.

The fight they are engaged in has been brutal. IS atrocities are the most notorious and egregious, including mass killings of captured soldiers and civilians. But Shiite militias are said to have committed abuses as well. In February, Human Rights Watch accused individual Shiite militias under the Popular Mobilization Forces umbrella of "possible war crimes," including forcing Sunni civilians from their home and abducting and summarily executing them.

In June, the United Nations Children's Fund called for "urgent measures" to be taken by the Iraqi government to protect children, including criminalizing the recruitment of children and "the association of children with the Popular Mobilization Forces."

The U.S. State Department released its annual Trafficking in Persons report Monday in which it lists foreign governments identified over the past year as having armed forces or government-supported armed groups that recruit and use child soldiers. Those governments are subject to restrictions in the following fiscal year on certain security assistance and commercial licensing of military equipment. The report lists Syria, but not Iraq.

Donatella Rovera, Amnesty International's senior crisis response adviser, said that if the Shiite militias are using children as fighters, "then the countries that are supporting them are in violation of the U.N. Convention" on the Rights of the Child.

"If you are supporting the Iraqi army, then by extension, you are supporting the PMF," she said.

Iraq has a long history of training underage fighters. Under Saddam Hussein, boys 12 through 17 known as "Saddam's lion cubs" would attend monthlong training during summer breaks with the goal of eventually merging them into the Fadayeen - a paramilitary force loyal to Saddam's Baathist regime.

The Iraqi army restricts the age of its recruits to between 18 and 35, a policy that rights groups say is enforced. But there is no law governing the Popular Mobilization Forces. A draft law for the national guard, a force geared toward empowering Sunni tribes to police their own communities, purposely omits any age restrictions, lawmakers saying they want to open it to qualified fighters over age 35.

The U.N. convention does not ban giving military training to minors. But Jo Becker, the advocacy director of the children's rights division at Human Rights Watch, said that it puts children at risk.

"Governments like to say, 'Of course, we can recruit without putting children in harm's way,' but in a place of conflict, those landscapes blur very quickly," she said.

Once in a combat situation, children are plunged into the horrors of war, she said. "They don't have a mature sense of right and wrong and they may commit atrocities more easily than adults."

Chapter 4

FLIGHT OR FIGHT?

Displaced civilians from Ramadi and surrounding areas walk through Amiriyat al-Fallujah toward Baghdad, The United Nations World Food Program said it is rushing food assistance into Anbar to help tens of thousands of residents who have fled Ramadi after it was taken by the Islamic State militant group, May 22, 2015. (AP Photo/Hadi Mizban)

RAMADI GHOST TOWN
Baghdad, Iraq, Thursday, April 16, 2015

More than 2,000 families have fled the Iraqi city of Ramadi with little more than the clothes on their backs, officials said Thursday, as the Islamic State group closed in on the capital of western Anbar province, clashing with Iraqi troops and turning it into a ghost town.

The extremist group, which has controlled the nearby city of Fallujah for more than a year, captured three villages on Ramadi's eastern outskirts on Wednesday. The advance is widely seen as a counteroffensive after the Islamic State group lost the city of Tikrit, Saddam Hussein's hometown, earlier this month.

Hundreds of U.S. troops are training Iraqi forces at a military base west of Ramadi, but a U.S. military official said the fighting had no impact on the U.S. soldiers there, and that there were no plans to withdraw them.

The fleeing Ramadi residents were settling in the southern and western suburbs of Baghdad, and tents, food and other aid were being sent to them, said Sattar Nowruz, an official of the Ministry of Migration and the Displaced.

The ministry was assessing the situation with the provincial government in order "to provide the displaced people, who are undergoing difficult conditions, with better services and help," Nowruz said.

Sporadic clashes were still underway Thursday, according to security officials in Ramadi. Government forces control the city center, while the IS group has had a presence in the suburbs and outskirts for months. They described Ramadi as a ghost town, with empty streets and closed shops.

Video obtained by The Associated Press showed plumes of thick, black smoke billowing above the city as fighter jets pounded militant targets. On the city outskirts, displaced residents frantically tried to make their way out amid the heavy bombardment.

U.S.-led coalition airstrikes targeted the IS group in Sjariyah, Albu-Ghanim and Soufiya, the three villages the extremists captured Wednesday, the officials added. They spoke on condition of anonymity because they were not allowed to talk to the media.

Anbar's deputy governor, Faleh al-Issawi, described the situation in Ramadi as "catastrophic" and urged the central government to send in reinforcements.

"We urge the Baghdad government to supply us immediately with troops and weapons in order to help us prevent the city from falling into the hands of the IS group," he told the Associated Press in a telephone interview.

The spokesman for the U.N. secretary-general, Stephane Dujarric, said access to the city was limited but humanitarian workers were trying to verify the reports of fleeing residents. Prior to the current bout of fighting, some 400,000 Iraqis were already displaced, including 60,000 in Ramadi district, according to the International Organization for Migration.

Al-Bayan, the Islamic State group's English-language radio station, claimed IS fighters had seized control of at least six areas and most of a seventh to the east of Ramadi since Wednesday, according to the SITE Intelligence Group, which monitors militant websites.

American troops fought some of their bloodiest battles in Anbar during the eight-year U.S. intervention, when Fallujah and Ramadi were strongholds of al-Qaida in Iraq, a precursor to the IS group. Fallujah was the first Iraqi city to fall to the militants, in January 2014.

Masked Sunni protesters wave Islamist flags while others chant slogans at an anti-government rally in Fallujah, August 26, 2013. (AP Photo/Bilal Fawzi)

Iraqi Prime Minister Haider al-Abadi, who was visiting Washington on Wednesday, made no mention of the events in Ramadi. Instead he spoke optimistically about recruiting Sunni tribal fighters to battle the extremists, saying about 5,000 such fighters in Anbar had signed up and received light weapons.

The IS-run Al-Bayan station also reported that an attempt by Iraqi troops to advance on the Beiji oil refinery in Salahuddin province, about 250 kilometers (115 miles) north of Baghdad, was pushed back and that fighters "positioned themselves in multiple parts of the refinery after taking control of most of it," according to SITE.

Iraqi officials could not immediately be reached for comment on the fighting around Beiji. On Monday, Oil Minister Adel Abdul-Mahdi said that Iraqi forces, backed by U.S.-led coalition airstrikes, had repelled an IS attack on Beiji over the weekend.

Meanwhile, a senior U.S. military official told The Associated Press that there were no plans to evacuate U.S. troops from the Ain al-Asad air base, about 110 kilometers (70 miles) west of Ramadi - and stressed that the current fighting around Ramadi had no impact on the base. He spoke on condition of anonymity because he was not authorized to talk to the media.

Since January, hundreds of U.S. forces have been training Iraqi troops at the base.

THE BZEBIZ BRIDGE
On the Bzebiz Bridge, Iraq, Tuesday, April 21, 2015

In the two weeks since militants from the Islamic State group overran central Ramadi, thousands of people have streamed out of the city, fleeing the brutal clashes between the extremists and Iraqi security forces.

With the announcement late Monday that the Iraqi military has retaken key areas in and around the city, the tide has suddenly shifted: Thousands are turning around and heading back toward Ramadi, turning this rickety, makeshift bridge over the Euphrates River into a scene of chaos and clogged traffic.

Through the heat and blinding dust, men and women loaded down with suitcases and bags crossed the bridge west of Baghdad on Tuesday. Some led livestock on ropes. Others pushed carts carrying children or the elderly and a few meager possessions.

Many said they had nowhere to go. In war-weary Iraq, residents of cities like Baghdad view the mostly Sunni residents of Anbar province with suspicion.

One man who was still headed away from Ramadi, the capital of Anbar province, bellowed a warning to those who were streaming back toward it.

"Turn around!" he cautioned as he crossed into Baghdad province. "It's not safe!"

Iraqi security forces - supported by airstrikes from a U.S.-led coalition - have been making gains in recent weeks to take back territory seized last year by extremists from the self-described Islamic

State. Iraqi troops were fresh off a victory last month in the city of Tikrit when the militants pushed into Ramadi, prompting some 114,000 residents to run, according to the U.N.

Displaced Iraqis from Ramadi cross the Bzebiz Bridge fleeing fighting in Ramadi. Thousands of displaced people fleeing violence in nearby Anbar province poured into Baghdad province after the central government granted them conditional entry, May 20, 2015. (AP Photo/ Karim Kadim)

Buoyed by the strong air campaign and volunteer fighters, the military made a quick and decisive response in Ramadi. Still, residents took no chances and fled the city in unprecedented numbers.

In the days that followed, however, some changed their minds and believed they were better off at home.

That has spurred the frantic two-way traffic on the bridge - a temporary structure erected in place of one bombed by the militants. The new one was meant to support no more than the occasional fruit-and-vegetable cart heading for Baghdad, whose outskirts are about 65 kilometers (40 miles) to the east.

"We now have more people returning (to Anbar) than those coming," said army Brigadier General Abdullah Jareh Wahib.

Ambulances were stationed at both ends of the bridge, providing assistance to those who had walked for miles under the intense sun. The bridge rocked over the river's current as residents made their way across.

"We never expected that within a month's time, tens of thousands of people would be crossing the bridge," said Wahib. "The bridge wasn't built for this kind of weight."

Militants from the Islamic State group with truckloads of captured Iraqi soldiers after taking over a base in Tikrit. Iraq won the battle to retake the city of Tikrit from the Islamic State group, backed by a coalition of the unlikely in Iranian advisers, Shiite militias and U.S.-led airstrikes, but the country now faces what could be its most important battle: Winning the support of the Sunni, June 14, 2014. (AP Photo/Militant Website)

More than 1,000 people trying to cross the bridge Sunday into Baghdad province were stopped at the span, the U.N. said Tuesday. Provincial officials were requiring a sponsor to vouch for them before they were admitted to enter Baghdad or allowed to travel toward Iraq's northern Kurdish region, because of fears they may be members of the Islamic State group. Babil province has also prohibited male residents of Anbar province aged 18-50 from entering without similar guarantees.

"We understand that there are members of Daesh trying to infiltrate the province via these displaced people," said Hassan Fedaam, a member of the Babil provincial council, using an Arabic acronym for the IS group.

Saif Mohammed Abbas, 21, evacuated his family last week, but he was among the thousands heading back to Ramadi on Tuesday.

"Mortars were hitting our home and falling on us, so it wasn't safe for them," he said. "But I have to go back. Someone has to look after our home; otherwise, it might get taken or destroyed in the fighting."

Others said they couldn't bear to live in squalor at refugee camps that have struggled to keep up with the growing number of displaced. Some said that for the poorest of Ramadi residents, there are no good choices.

Displaced people from Ramadi cross Bzebiz Bridge, April 18, 2015. (AP Photo/Karim Kadim)

"The poor are in trouble," said Ahmed Saddam, owner of a utilities store in the city. "They have no options. The camps are miserable and life in Ramadi is unbearable."

Thousands continue to pour out of Ramadi, preferring to take no chances as gunfire and airstrikes continue relentlessly.

"Conditions are worsening," said Adrian Edwards, a spokesman for the U.N. refugee agency. "The newly displaced are exhausted. Some people have walked many miles without food or water."

Sabiha Maalim, a woman from the town of Habani, had left her home on Tuesday, saying the IS militants are the least of her worries.

"There were rockets firing all night," she said. "Daesh is hitting the military. The military is hitting Daesh. And we are in the middle. We don't know what our future is."

An Iraqi refugee girl imitates holding a camera, as she stands outside her tent at a camp for displaced Iraqis who fled from Mosul and other towns, in the Khazer area outside Irbil, June 22, 2014. (AP Photo/Hussein Malla)

Chapter 5

STRANGER THAN FICTION

Ahmed Hassan, a reality show host, center right, stands next to Haider Ali Motar, as the TV crew films "In the Grip of the Law," a reality show produced by Iraqi state TV, in Baghdad. Motar was convicted of terrorism charges about a month ago for helping to carry out a string of Baghdad car bombings on behalf of the Islamic State extremist group. Now, the 21-year old is a reluctant cast member in the reality TV show, December 16, 2014. (AP Photo/Hadi Mizban)

REMOVING WOMEN FROM PUBLIC LIFE
Beirut, Lebanon, Tuesday, December 23, 2014

The gunmen came to the all-girls' elementary school in the Iraqi city of Fallujah at midday with a special delivery: piles of long black robes with gloves and face veils, now required dress code for females in areas ruled by the Islamic State group.

"These are the winter version. Make sure every student gets one," one of the men told a supervisor at the school earlier this month.

Extremists are working to excise women from public life across the territory controlled by the Islamic State group, stretching hundreds of kilometers (miles) from the outskirts of the Syrian city of Aleppo in the west to the edges of the Iraqi capital in the east.

The group has been most notorious for its atrocities, including the horrors it inflicted on women and girls from Iraq's minority Yazidi community when its fighters overran their towns this year. Hundreds of Yazidi women and girls were abducted and given to extremists as slaves. A report by Amnesty International released Tuesday said the captives - including girls as young as 10-12 - endured torture, rape and sexual slavery, and that several abducted girls committed suicide.

In day-to-day life, the group has also dramatically hemmed in women's lives across the Sunni Muslim heartland that makes up the bulk of Islamic State group territory, activists and residents say. Their movements are restricted and their opportunity for work has shrunk.

In Iraq's Mosul, the biggest city in the group's self-declared caliphate, "life for women has taken a 180-degree turn," said Hanaa Edwer, a prominent Iraqi human rights activist. "They are forbidding them from learning, forbidding them from moving around freely. The appearance of a woman is being forcefully altered."

At least eight women have been stoned to death for alleged adultery in IS-controlled areas in northern Syria, activists say.

At least 10 women in Mosul have been killed for speaking out against the group, Edwer said. In August, IS detained and beheaded a female dentist in Deir el-Zour who had continued to treat patients of both sexes, the U.N. said.

Relatives of women considered improperly dressed or found in the company of males who are not relatives are lashed or imprisoned. In the IS-controlled town of al-Bab in Syria's northern Aleppo province, an activist described seeing armed militants walking with a stick in hand, gently whacking or jabbing at women deemed inappropriately dressed.

"Sometimes they follow the woman home and detain her father, or they confiscate her ID and tell her to come back with her father to pick it up," said Bari Abdelatif, now based in Turkey.

Displaced Iraqi woman wearing a khimar with a niqah veil over her face, May 16, 2015. (AP Photo/Hadi Mizban)

Enforcement varies from one place to the other, much of it depending on the whims of the Hisba, or vice police enforcing those rules. Most of the areas taken over by IS were already deeply conservative places where women had a subordinate role in society, but the extremists have sharply exacerbated the restrictions.

Abdelatif said women in al-Bab are harassed for venturing outside their home without a "mahram," or male guardian. In the Syrian city of Raqqa, the militants' de facto capital, activists said women were allowed to leave their homes on their own, but needed a male companion or permission of a male relative to leave the city.

An IS all-female brigade, called al-Khansa, patrols the streets in some areas to enforce clothing restrictions.

Across the territory, women now have to wear the "khimar," a tent-like robe that covers the head, shoulders and chest. The khimar leaves the face exposed but very often the militants go ahead and force women to put a niqab veil over their faces as well, leaving only the eyes visible.

In the Iraqi city of Fallujah, an elementary school teacher said militants recently dropped by the school to deliver the niqab, robes and gloves for the students to wear.

"I used to wear make-up on occasion but I don't anymore," she said, speaking by phone on strict condition of anonymity for fear of reprisals.

The militants have segregated schools and changed the curriculum. In some cases they shut schools down, summoning teachers to take a course in their hardline version of Islamic Shariah law before reopening them. In many instances in both Iraq and Syria, parents have opted not to send their children to school to avoid IS brainwashing them.

Hospitals have also been segregated. A woman has to be seen by a female doctor, but there are very few women doctors left.

Early marriage is on the rise because parents want to find husbands for their daughters quickly for fear they will be forced to marry Islamic State fighters, according to the U.N.

"The psychological and physical harm caused by ISIS's treatment of women, the onerous instructions imposed on their dress code, and restrictions on their freedom of movement demonstrate discriminatory treatment on the basis of gender," a United Nations panel investigating war crimes in the Syrian conflict said last month.

It said the killings and acts of sexual violence perpetrated by IS constitute crimes against humanity.

While the Islamic State group imposes its extremist vision of Islamic law on Sunni Muslim women under its rule, it went further when it overran the Iraqi villages of the Yazidi minority in early August. The extremists consider followers of the Yazidi faith as infidels - and thus permissible to enslave.

Amnesty International interviewed more than 40 former captives who escaped the militants and described being abducted, raped and being "sold" or given as "gifts" to Islamic State fighters or supporters.

Syrian woman Rasha Abdoullah, 24, who fled with her family from Raqqa in Syria, sits in her tent, as she holds her two-month-old daughter Sham at a Syrian refugee camp in the village of Riyak in the eastern Bekaa Valley, Lebanon, September 10, 2014. (AP Photo/Bilal Hussein)

One girl told how a 19-year-old among them named Jilan committed suicide, fearing rape.

In the bathroom, "she cut her wrists and hanged herself. She was very beautiful," the girl quoted in the report said. "I think she knew she was going to be taken away by a man."

A NOT SO GREAT CALIPHATE
Baghdad, Iraq, Saturday, December 13, 2014

Saadi Abdul-Rahman was recently forced to pull his three children out of school in the Iraqi city of Mosul, where Islamic State militants have ruled with an iron fist since June. The cost of living has soared there, and the family is barely able to make ends meet, even after putting the kids to work.

"We are not able to pay for cooking gas, kerosene and food," laments the 56-year-old retired government worker. "The situation in Mosul is miserable."

The economy in the self-styled "caliphate" declared by the Islamic State group bridging Iraq and Syria is starting to show signs of strain. Prices of most staples have more than doubled as coalition airstrikes make it difficult for products to move in and out of militant strongholds, leading to shortages, price-gouging and the creation of black markets.

Resentment has grown among residents under the rule of the extremists, who initially won support with their ability to deliver services.

In the early days of its rule, the Islamic State group subsidized food and gas prices through the wealth it accumulated from oil smuggling, extortion and ransom demands. They sold their smuggled oil at a discount- $25 to $60 a barrel for oil that normally cost $100 a barrel or more, according to analysts and government officials.

But in recent weeks, prices have soared in militant-held cities. Items like kerosene, used for heating and cooking, are in short supply, while others, such as alcohol and cigarettes, strictly banned by the group, are making a comeback at higher prices on the black market.

Smoking is a punishable offense in militant-held Mosul. But at a warehouse on the outskirts of the city, cigarettes, as well as hard-to-come-by essentials like kerosene, can be found at hugely inflated prices on a black market run by the extremists. There, a pack of cigarettes sells for 30,000 dinars - the equivalent of $26 - more than double the pre-caliphate price, according to residents who spoke on condition of anonymity for fear of reprisals.

The militants "are developing an unsustainable economy," said Paul Sullivan, an expert on Middle East economies at the National Defense University in Washington. "Eventually the costs of keeping the subsidies and price controls going will overpower their smuggling funds, which are also used for offensive and defensive actions."

"They can collect taxes, extort money, and so forth," he said. "But that will likely not be enough in the long run to keep such an unbalanced economic system going."

In the Syrian city of Raqqa, the extremists' so-called capital, the breakdown of security along the border with Iraq in areas under Islamic State control has led to flourishing trade with Mosul. Trucks are also able to access the city from Turkey, allowing for a steady supply of fruit and vegetables, wheat and textiles. However, the cost of living has surged since U.S.-led airstrikes began in September, and power and water cuts grew more frequent, residents said.

In addition, the strict social laws imposed by the group have been very bad for business, said Bari Abdelatif, an activist in the Islamic State-controlled town of al-Bab in Syria's northern Aleppo province. But, he said, foreign fighters were bringing with them lots of hard currency, making up somewhat for the shortfall.

Last month, Abu Bakr al-Baghdadi, the leader of the Islamic State group, decreed the minting of gold, silver and copper coins for the militants' own currency - the Islamic dinar - to "change the tyrannical monetary system" modelled on Western economies. But trade in most militant-held cities continues to be in Iraqi dinars and U.S. dollars.

The start of winter has led to serious shortages of gasoline and kerosene. The official price for a liter of gas in government-controlled areas of Iraq is 450 dinars (40 cents) - but in Mosul, it sells for four times that. Two hundred-liter barrels of kerosene are now sold in Mosul for 250,000 dinars ($220), versus the official price of 30,000 dinars.

In the western Iraqi city of Fallujah, under militant control for almost a year, residents have started cutting trees for firewood because kerosene is in such short supply. The city is surrounded by government troops and near-daily shelling often make parts of town too dangerous to visit.

Food and fuel prices have risen sharply as a result - a 50-kilo sack of rice costs 75,000 dinars ($65), up from 10,000 ($9) three months ago. A cylinder of cooking gas goes for 140,000 dinars ($115).

That has put many staples out of reach for Abdul-Rahman and his family in Mosul, even with the additional money brought in by his sons, who left school to drive a taxi and work in a restaurant.

A number of factors are driving the shortages and price hikes, according to residents in Mosul and Fallujah, the group's biggest Iraqi strongholds. The militants have imposed a tax on vehicles entering their territory, leading to a decline in business. Deliveries are also subject to militant theft, and coalition airstrikes and military operations make many roads impassable.

A woman looks at damage from a car bomb attack near a Kebab restaurant, in the mainly Shiite Habibiya neighborhood of Baghdad, Iraq. A series of bombings in Iraq killed and wounded scores of people, a day after army shelling killed many civilians and gunmen in the militant-held city of Fallujah, May 11, 2014. (AP Photo/Karim Kadim)

As a result, the trip from the Turkish border to Mosul took four hours prior to the militant takeover. Now, a delivery truck can spend as much as a week traveling the same road, and will pay a tax of as much as $300 for entry into Mosul, residents said.

According to Luay al-Khateeb, director of the Iraqi Energy Institute and a visiting fellow at the Brookings Doha Center, the population of the areas under Islamic State control in Iraq and Syria is 6.5 million to 8 million people.

"They need 150,000 barrels (of crude) a day just to meet local consumption," he said. "And that is the bare minimum to meet the demands for transportation, bakeries, power generation."

"That doesn't mean they have access to such supply," he added.

Last month, the militants shut down cell phone service in Mosul, claiming that residents were tipping off U.S.-led airstrikes to their whereabouts. Cell signals have not been restored, causing the city to come to a virtual standstill. Workshops, factories and markets are closed and bitterness is growing among business owners.

"Most money-transfer operations are done by mobile calls," said Osama Abdul-Aziz, the owner of a money-transfer office in Mosul. "We have the option of using the Internet, but this method is very slow and sometimes the Internet does not work at all, which causes big delays to our work."

At Mohammed Abdullah's shop in Mosul, the pile of cell phone scratch cards is growing higher by the day. "Our business and means for living are in ruins now," he said.

IRAQI REALITY TV
Baghdad, Iraq, Monday, December 22, 2014

Haider Ali Motar was convicted of terrorism charges about a month ago for helping to carry out a string of Baghdad car bombings on behalf of the Islamic State extremist group. Now, the 21-year old is a reluctant cast member in a popular reality TV show.

"In the Grip of the Law," brings convicted terrorists face-to-face with victims in surreal encounters and celebrates the country's beleaguered security forces. The show, produced by state-run Iraqiyya TV, is among dozens of programs, cartoons and musical public service announcements aimed at shoring up support for the troops after their humiliating defeat last summer at the hands of the Islamic State group, which now controls about a third of the country.

On a chilly, overcast day last week, the crew arrived at the scene of one of the attacks for which Motar was convicted, with a heavily armed escort in eight military pick-up trucks and Humvees. Passing cars clogged the road to watch the drama unfold, but were quickly shooed away by soldiers.

After being pulled from an armored vehicle, a shackled Motar found himself face-to-face with the seething relatives of the victims of the attack. "Give him to me - I'll tear him to pieces," one of the relatives roared from behind a barbed wire barrier.

A cameraman pinned a microphone on Motar's bright yellow prison jumpsuit as he stood alongside a busy Baghdad highway looking bewildered by his surroundings.

"Say something," the cameraman said to him.

"What am I supposed to say?" a visibly panicked Motar asked.

"It's a mic check! Just count: 1,2,3,4..."

Ahmed Hassan, a reality show host, center, stands next to Haider Ali Motar, left, who was performing for "In the Grip of the Law", December 16, 2014. (AP Photo/Hadi Mizban)

Once the cameras were rolling, the show's host Ahmed Hassan quizzed the still-shackled prisoner. When Motar was confronted by one of the victims, a young man in a wheelchair who lost his father in one of the attacks, the convict began weeping, as the cameras rolled.

Iraq has seen near-daily car bombs and other attacks for more than a decade, both before and after the withdrawal of U.S.-led troops at the end of 2011. But the central message of the show, the filming of which began last year, is that the security forces will bring perpetrators to justice.

"We wanted to produce a program that offers clear and conclusive evidence, with the complete story, presented and shown to Iraqi audiences," Hassan told The Associated Press. "Through surveillance videos, we show how the accused parked the car, how he blew it up, how he carries out an assassination."

The episodes often detail the trail of evidence that led security forces to make the arrest. Police allow the camera crew to film the evidence - explosive belts, bomb-making equipment or fingerprints and other DNA samples.

"We show our audiences the pictures, along with hard evidence, to leave no doubts that this person is a criminal and paying for his crimes," Hassan said.

Life and Death in ISIS

A man, center, expresses his anger at Haider Ali Motar, not seen, as they perform a scene from "In the Grip of the Law." The man is a relative of a victim who was killed in an attack for which Motar was convicted, December 16, 2014. (AP Photo/Hadi Mizban)

All of the alleged terrorists are shown confessing to their crimes in one-on-one interviews. Hassan said the episodes are only filmed after the men have confessed to a judge, insisting it is "impossible" that any of them are innocent.

"The court first takes a preliminary testimony and then they require a legal confession in front of a judge," Hassan explained. "After obtaining the security and legal permission, we are then allowed to film those terrorists."

Human rights groups have long expressed concern over the airing of confessions by prisoners, many of whom have been held incommunicado in secret facilities.

"The justice system is so flawed and the rights of detainees, especially those accused of terrorism (but not only) are so routinely violated that it is virtually impossible to be confident that they would be able to speak freely," Donatella Rovera, of Amnesty International, said in an email.

"In recent months, which I have spent in Iraq, virtually every family I have met who has a relative detained has complained that they do not have access to them, and the same is true for lawyers."

In a September statement, Amnesty cited longstanding concerns about the Iraqi justice system, "where many accused of terrorism have been convicted and sentenced to long prison terms and even to death on the basis of 'confessions" extracted under torture."

Such concerns are rarely if ever aired on Iraqi TV, where wall-to-wall programming exalts the security forces. Singers embedded with the troops sing nationalist songs during commercial breaks. In another popular program, called "The Quick Response," a traveling correspondent interviews soldiers, aiming to put a human face on the struggle against the extremists.

Iraqi forces backed by Shiite and Kurdish militias, as well as U.S.-led coalition airstrikes, have clawed back some territory following the army's route last summer, when commanders disappeared, calls for reinforcements went unanswered and many soldiers stripped off their uniforms and fled. But around a third of the country - including its second largest city, Mosul - remains under the firm control of militants, and nearly every day brings new bombings in and around the capital.

Back at the makeshift barricade set up for "In the Grip of the Law," security officials insist they are nevertheless sending a message of deterrence.

"Many of these terrorists feel a lot of remorse when they see the victims," said the senior intelligence officer overseeing the shoot, who declined to be named since he often works undercover. "When people see that, it makes them think twice about crossing the law."

SHIITE FIGHTERS
Baghdad, Iraq, Saturday, December 20, 2014

Abu Murtada al-Moussawi answered the call last summer from Iraq's top Shiite cleric to help save the country from the Islamic State group, but after less than three months on the front lines he and several friends returned home because they had run out of food.

"Sometimes, we didn't have enough money to buy mobile scratch cards to call our families," al-Moussawi, a Shiite from the southern city of Basra, said. "Everybody felt like we were being forgotten by the government."

Now Iraq's Shiite religious establishment is urging the faithful to donate food, money and supplies. The clerics hope to prevent a repeat of last summer's collapse of Iraq's demoralized army in the face of the Islamic State group's lightning advance, which saw the extremists capture the country's second largest city Mosul and sweep south toward the capital.

Shortly after the June blitz across northern Iraq, tens of thousands of Shiite men answered a nationwide call-to-arms by the top Shiite cleric, Grand Ayatollah Ali al-Sistani. Many volunteers came from the country's most impoverished areas and were barely able to make ends meet even before taking up arms.

The Shiite fighters are credited with helping to stall the militants' advance outside Baghdad, breaking the siege of the northern Shiite-majority town of Amirli in August, and later driving the militants out of Jurf al-Sakher south of the capital.

Iraqi Shiite fighters make their way to the front line to fight militants from the extremist Islamic State group in Jurf al-Sakhar, 43 miles south of Baghdad, August 18, 2014. (AP Photo/Hadi MIzban)

Al-Moussawi was deployed along with fellow militiamen in Latifiyah, a town 30 kilometers (20 miles) south of Baghdad, with orders to keep the Islamic State group out of Sunni areas along the so-called Baghdad Belt. But over the past two months, the number of men in al-Moussawi's unit has dwindled, with as many as 1,000 deserting over economic hardship, he said.

In the upscale Baghdad neighborhood of Harthiya, a representative from al-Sistani's office recently urged his followers to donate food and money to the Shiite militias - warning that many fighters had already deserted.

He said that instead of spending money on cooking the traditional large meals to mark a recent holiday, Shiites should instead donate to front-line militiamen. Since then, donations of money, clothing and food have begun pouring into the local Shiite mosque and charity office.

Iraq Shiite fighters make their way to the front line to fight militants from the extremist Islamic State group in Jurf al-Sakhar, 43 miles south of Baghdad, August 18, 2014. (AP Photo/Hadi MIzban)

Issam Abbas said he and other merchants in Basra have begun sending four truckloads of food and water to the front lines each month as their contribution to the war against the Islamic State group.

"I and other traders cannot leave our businesses, so we consider our monthly donations as a jihad against the terrorists," he said.

In the Baghdad Shiite stronghold of Sadr City, desperately-needed ammunition is being purchased through donations by wealthy Shiites. The drive to send weapons to the Shiite fighters has pushed the price of a single bullet from 40 cents to about $2, while an AK-47 is now sold for $800 compared to just $350 a few months ago.

Hassan Saleh, owner of a cafe in Sadr City, took part in battles against the IS group north of Baghdad in September. But he and his fellow militiamen never received any financial support from the government and depended completely on donations and their own money to meet their daily needs, he said. In early October, he returned home to look after his family.

"The government's negligence toward us has created bitterness among the volunteer fighters risking their lives in order to protect the country," he said. "We did not receive any salary, while the government is continuing to pay the salaries of the soldiers and the policemen who abandoned their positions without fighting in June."

GHOST SOLDIERS
Baghdad, Iraq, Tuesday, December 16, 2014

The Iraqi government has identified and stopped payment of tens of millions of dollars in salaries previously disbursed to nonexistent troops, known here as "ghost soldiers," as part of the prime minister's vow to tackle corruption in the military and regain a foothold in the battle against the Islamic State group, two senior government officials said.

The initiative is part of Prime Minister Haider al-Abadi's plan to rebuild the U.S.-trained military which crumbled in the face of last summer's onslaught by Islamic State militants.

Al-Abadi recently purged the military and interior ministry from a number of senior officials who were appointees of his predecessor, Nouri al-Maliki. While it is unclear whether any of the sacked officials are among those accused of collecting misappropriated funds, al-Abadi vowed to pursue the sensitive matter "even if it costs me my life."

According to the two senior officials, authorities prevented the loss of over $47 million of improper military spending in November, mostly from salaries that were previously paid to soldiers who are dead, missing or did not exist and which were pocketed by senior commanders. The two officials, who spoke on condition of anonymity because they are not authorized to speak to media, said the money was the first of several tranches of funding to be regained by Iraq's Defense Ministry.

Iraqi prime Minister Haider al-Abadi, speaks at a press conference Baghdad, Iraq, Dec. 17, 2014. (AP Photo/Karim Kadim)

Al-Abadi announced last month that at least 50,000 ghost soldiers existed in four different divisions of the military and would be cut from its payroll. "We were paying salaries while we lack the money," he said in a televised address.

"We have started blowing some big fish out of the water and we'll go after them until the end," he added.

The Iraqi military has struggled to recover from its collapse in June when the Islamic State group captured the country's second largest city, Mosul, and swept over much of northern Iraq. In the face of the blitz, commanders disappeared. Pleas for more ammunition went unanswered. In some cases, soldiers stripped off their uniforms and ran.

The Iraqi army has since been reduced to 10 of the 14 divisions it had before the Islamic State offensive in June. The government officially says the country's total military and police forces stand at 1 million men. However, a senior Iraqi military official told The Associated Press that the military consisted of 238,000 fighters as of early December.

That figure is overstated, according to a senior U.S. military official, who said Iraqi military strength stands, generously, at 125,000 - down from 205,000 in January 2014. He believes the number of ghost soldiers is far greater than the 50,000 cited by the prime minister, but did not give his own estimate. Both military officials also spoke on condition of anonymity because they were not authorized to speak to media.

If all 50,000 soldiers cited by the prime minister received an entry-level salary (about $750 per month), it would add up to at least $450 million in bogus salaries per year.

"The numbers will be much higher if the investigation includes ghost policemen in the Interior Ministry," Iraqi lawmaker Liqaa Wardi told the AP. "I think that the efforts exerted by the current government will face resistance by some corrupt army and security officers who have made gains and fortunes due to the corruption system and the ghost soldiers."

Many have blamed the army's poor performance on al-Maliki, saying he replaced top officers with inexperienced or incompetent political allies in order to monopolize power. From 2010 until his resignation in August, al-Maliki had also held both the interior and defense portfolios, in part because lawmakers could not agree on nominees for them.

In the case of the fall of Mosul, poor training and a lack of loyalty to the central government have been widely cited as a principle cause for the military's collapse there.

Once al-Abadi was sworn in and his government approved, it took six weeks to fill the critical posts of interior and defense ministers following a deadlock among rival parliamentary blocs.

The U.S., which began airstrikes on August 8 to reinforce Iraqi and Kurdish forces, is now looking to boost its efforts with additional weapons supplies to the embattled Iraqi military. The Pentagon has made a spending request to Congress of $1.6 billion, focusing on training and arming Iraqi and Kurdish forces. According to a Pentagon document prepared last month, the U.S. is looking to provide an estimated $89.3 million worth of weapons and other equipment to each of the nine Iraqi army brigades.

Part of the drive to target the ghost soldier corruption is also financial necessity. Plunging oil prices and soaring costs from Iraq's war against the Islamic State group have taken a significant toll on Iraq's economy, prompting government spending cuts, including in defense, which so far constitutes 22 percent of next year's proposed budget, according to Finance Minister Hoshyar Zebari.

"Any senior military official involved in such obvious corrosive corruption should be court martialed and tossed in jail - especially in a perilous environment such as that which Iraq is facing," said Paul Sullivan, an expert on Middle East affairs at National Defense University in Washington. "The regular people and the lower ranks are hurt the most by the corruption of the leaders."

Chapter 6

MEDIA WARS

A computer screen is pictured at TV5 Monde after the French television network was hacked by people claiming allegiance to the Islamic State group, in Paris, France. The hackers briefly cut transmission of 11 channels belonging to TV5 Monde and took over its websites and social media accounts, April 9, 2015. (AP Photo/Christophe Ena)

GLOSSY MAGAZINES AND SLICK SOCIAL MEDIA
Dubai, United Arab Emirates, Sunday, September 21, 2014

As the Islamic State group battles across Syria and Iraq, pushing back larger armies and ruling over entire cities, it is also waging an increasingly sophisticated media campaign that has rallied disenfranchised youth and outpaced the sluggish efforts of Arab governments to stem its appeal.

Long gone are the days when militant leaders like Osama bin Laden smuggled grainy videos to Al-Jazeera. Nowadays Islamic State backers use Twitter, Facebook and other online platforms to entice recruits with professionally made videos showing fighters waging holy war and building an Islamic utopia.

The extremist group's opponents say it is dragging the region back into the Middle Ages with its grisly beheadings and massacres, but its tech-savvy media strategy has exposed the ways in which Arab governments and mainstream religious authorities seem to be living in the past.

Most Arab governments see social media as a threat to their stability and have largely failed to harness its power, experts say. Instead, they have tried to monitor and censor the Internet while churning out stale public statements and state-approved sermons on stuffy government-run media.

Last week, Saudi Arabia's top council of religious scholars issued a lengthy Arabic statement via the state-run news agency denouncing terrorism and calling on citizens to back efforts to fight extremist groups like the Islamic State and al-Qaida. Leading Sunni Muslim authorities in Egypt have issued similar government-backed statements.

Compare that to the Islamic State group. Its Furqan media arm produces slick videos complete with interviews, graphics and jihadist hymns echoing in the background, with Arabic and English subtitles. It promotes the videos and its glossy monthly magazines on an array of social media, reaching out to people in the Arab world and beyond. Islamic State fighters even tweet live from the battlefield, giving real-time updates and waging theological debates with online detractors.

"They definitely have an electronic army behind them," said Ray Kafity, vice president of FireEye for the Middle East, Turkey and Africa. The company manufactures IT solutions for defending against cyber threats.

The Islamic State boasts thousands of foreign fighters, some of whom were first drawn to it in the privacy and security of cyberspace. It also uses social media for fundraising.

Fadi Salem, a Dubai-based researcher on Internet governance in the Arab World, said the immediate response of Middle Eastern governments to the power of social media has been to "control, block and censor as much as possible."

"Very few governments viewed this as an opportunity rather than a risk," Salem said.

Life and Death in ISIS

The U.S. and Emirati governments said they have launched a new digital communications center focused on using social media to counter the Islamic State group's active online propaganda efforts. The new Sawab Center, based in Abu Dhabi, became operational, July 8, 2015. (AP Photo/Kamran Jebreili)

Egypt shut down access to the Internet during the bloodiest day of the 2011 uprising that toppled President Hosni Mubarak, and Syria cut off access in rebellious provinces shortly after the start of the revolt against Bashar Assad later that spring.

Iraq's government followed suit in June of this year, when the Islamic State group swept across much of the country's north and west. The government cut off Internet access to several areas overrun by militants, including Mosul, Iraq's second largest city.

A study by The Citizen Lab at the University of Toronto showed that despite blocking mobile messaging apps and social media platforms, Iraq's authorities failed to block seven websites affiliated with or supportive of the Islamic State group. New accounts appear almost as quickly as old accounts are reported and taken down.

"It's hard to wage a war with ideas online," said Abdulaziz Al-Mulhem, the spokesman for the Saudi Ministry of Information and Culture. "When we talk about monitoring or controlling social media it is like trying to control air, and this of course is hard."

Facebook says it has 71 million active monthly users in the Middle East, and youth between the ages of 15 and 29 make up around 70 percent of Facebook users in the Arab region, according to a report by the Dubai School of Government.

Facebook's Elizabeth Linder says Middle Eastern governments are still in the early stages of realizing the full potential of social media. She advises governments on how they can better use Facebook for diplomacy.

"The most important thing is to be there," she told The Associated Press on the sidelines of a social media conference in Dubai. "And that's something that I really do encourage governments to do, not to leave the space but to enter the space."

The United States, which has long struggled to craft an effective public diplomacy in the region, has taken note. The U.S. State Department launched a "Think Again Turn Away" campaign on YouTube, Facebook and Twitter, with Arabic and English videos similar in style to those of al-Qaida and the Islamic State group. One video is titled "Airing al-Qaida's dirty laundry" and another shows images of children allegedly killed by these groups.

But none have gained the traction of the Islamic State's videos, which pair brutal images of mass shootings and beheadings - aimed at striking fear in the hearts of its enemies - with heroic portrayals of its fighters as models of bravery and piety.

A slick 55-minute video entitled "Flames of War" came with its own trailer, and features images of exploding tanks and wounded U.S. soldiers. The video, which came out this month, was allegedly released by the Islamic State group's Al-Hayat media center. It idealizes militants as "warriors" and "truthful men."

The message to alienated young men in the region and abroad is that they too can wage holy war, exact revenge on those seen as oppressing Muslims and help build a just society based on divine law.

The videos that have gained the most attention in the West are those that show a masked man beheading two American journalists and a British aid worker in the desert. But others document life in militant-held Raqqa in eastern Syria, and cheerfully invite potential recruits to move there.

"We want to be your brothers and for you to be our brothers," an Islamic State fighter tells Syrian men and children in a video entitled "The best ummah" - or Muslim society.

The Arabic video with English subtitles depicts a community where pious men police the streets, eliminating drugs and alcohol and making sure everyone prays together at the mosque. The militants distribute food to those in need and ensure fair prices in the local markets.

Tunisian Islamic State extremist gunman Seifeddine Rezgui who killed tens of people in the Tunisian beach resort of Sousse, June 27, 2015. (AP Photo/Militant Website)

Head of the European Union's police agency Europol, Rob Wainwright, answers questions during an interview in The Hague, Netherlands. Rob Wainwright told The Associated Press a new unit at Europol will start fighting Islamic State propaganda and recruiters in cyberspace in a crackdown on the terror network's social media activities, January 16, 2015. (AP Photo/Peter Dejong)

For many it's a compelling vision of a better world, one that stands in stark contrast with most states in the region, in which aging autocrats preside over governments seen as irredeemably corrupt and stagnant. Combatting that vision will require more than simply silencing its advocates, experts say.

"Pure censorship and blocking is not really working. It will continue to be a cat-and-mouse game," Salem said. "Another way is to use these tools to attract people away from these ideas. A combination of both is required."

INSPIRING TERRORISM
New York, Sunday, September 21, 2014

The latest issue of the digital magazine "Dabiq" features glossy photos of smiling militants from the Islamic State group, mutilated bodies on the battlefield and articles with titles such as, "There is No Life Without Jihad" and "Foley's Blood is on Obama's Hands."

It refers to Americans as "crusaders" and "apostates." And it insists "sincere Muslims" must help speed "the complete collapse of the modern American empire."

Authorities say the magazine - published in English and other languages and easily available on the Internet - has become a potent propaganda tool for the group to recruit Westerners. They also warn that the publication, along with other inflammatory messages and videos on Twitter and other social media, have the power to incite so-called lone wolves who hatch domestic plots such as the ones officials have alleged recently in Australia and upstate New York.

"That is a current threat - their ability to inspire people here in the United States who can't travel to Syria to fight, or inspire people to travel to Syria and while they're there, train them and inspire them to come home and commit terrorist acts," New York Police Department Commissioner William Bratton said recently.

Australian authorities have detained suspects in an alleged plot to carry out random beheadings in Sydney. Across the globe, Mufid Elfgeeh, of Rochester, New York, pleaded not guilty to charges accusing him of trying to help three recruits get to the Mideast and plotting to kill members of the U.S. armed forces returning from war and Shiites in the Rochester area.

Australian Prime Minister Tony Abbott briefs media, in Sydney after police said they thwarted a plot to carry out beheadings in Australia by Islamic State group supporters when they raided more than a dozen properties across Sydney, September 19, 2014. (AP Photo/Rick Rycroft)

Terror propaganda on the Internet - and law enforcement's concern about it - isn't new: Since the September 11 attacks, the NYPD has assigned foreign-born officers fluent in languages like Arabic and Farsi to surf websites where hatred of the West rages as a way to detect threats. In 2007, it also released an analysis warning that the rants could put young men from the Middle East who had grown disillusioned with life in America on the path to jihad.

But authorities say the rise of the Islamic State group and the proliferation of al-Qaida offshoots has multiplied the anti-American messages found on the Internet, reaching an even broader audience and upping the potential to invite mayhem.

"ISIS and al-Qaida now are competing to see who can do the most," said Jerome Hauer, commissioner of the New York State Division of Homeland Security, using one of the acronyms for the group. "I think ISIS will become a greater threat as time goes on. ... But I don't see it as an organized attack. I see it as a 'lone wolf' attack."

One posting that surfaced last week - titled "To the Lone Wolves in America: How to Make a Bomb in Your Kitchen, to Create Scenes of Horror in Tourist Spots and Other Targets" - was purportedly sanctioned by the Islamic State group. Local authorities are less concerned about whether the posts are authentic and more so about whether they help radicalize homegrown terrorists, said John Miller, the NYPD's top counterterrorism official.

"When you talk about threats over social media, the business end is not on where the information originates, it's on the user end," Miller said. "It's calling on these lone wolves to take this information and carry out individual attacks."

The first edition of "Inspire" - another online magazine linked to an al-Qaida affiliate and known for publishing recipes for homemade bombs and recommending domestic targets - was found downloaded on the computer of one of the two brothers accused in the Boston Marathon bombing, authorities have said. A later edition after the attack proclaimed, "The act of the two great brothers ... is but the true image reflected by the bloody deeds of your hands, reflected by the oppressive policies of your downtrodding regimes."

The content of "Dabiq," named after a city in northern Syria, relies on religious texts to justify the caliphate and its religious authority over all Muslims. The latest edition blames President Barack Obama for the beheading of U.S. journalist James Foley by refusing to negotiate for his release, and accuses America of hypocrisy.

American Journalist James Foley, of Rochester, N.H., as he posed for a photo in Boston, May 27, 2011. (AP Photo/Steven Senne)

"If a mujahid kills a single man with a knife, it is the barbaric killing of the 'innocent,'" read one article. "However, if Americans kill thousands of Muslim families all over the world by pressing missile fire buttons, it's merely 'collateral damage.'"

Authorities say Elfgeeh, 30, expressed similar frustrations. According to court papers, he was caught on tape complaining that the American military was killing women and children and that, "If you kill in the name of Allah, then you have defended our sanctities and avenged their blood."

"Dabiq" offers no particulars on where and how it's published. However, it does say, "The Dabiq team would like to hear back from its readers." There was no response to messages sent to email addresses listed as contacts.

BRITISH JIHADIS
Portsmouth, England, Tuesday, November 4, 2014

Royal Navy sailors used to swagger out of this great seaport at the zenith of the British Empire, manning the warships and trading vessels that made this nation rich and powerful. Today a handful of young men are again leaving to go to war - but this time they have sworn allegiance to foreign terrorists.

Bangladeshi community leader Syed Haque and chairman of the Jami Mosque's advisory council poses for a portrait for The Associated Press, in Portsmouth, England, October 31, 2014. (AP Photo/Alastair Grant)

It is a sign of the times that Portsmouth, with its tradition of naval glory, finds itself trying to persuade young British Muslims not to follow six locals who traveled to Syria to join forces with Islamic State extremists battling President Bashar Assad.

Numbers alone might be a deterrent: Four or the six are dead, one is in jail, and only one is still believed active on the battlefield. But police, political leaders and Islamic community activists believe those facts alone may not convince angry young men that joining the Islamic State group - which has declared Britain an enemy - will destroy their lives.

The front of the mosque most of the young men attended before departing for Syria is decorated with an elaborate mosaic that says: "Peace Is Better." Syed Haque, chairman of the Jami Mosque's advisory council, is mystified that some of the congregation has chosen war instead.

"All those boys went, they were university students, they were working," he said. "There was nothing in their faces showing they were miserable or had problems at home or weren't being looked after by their family."

"Everybody is talking about this now: How come we didn't know anything about it? Now that we know, what can we do? If those boys went, there could be other people thinking of doing it. How do we prevent that?"

Nationwide, British officials estimate that some 600 Britons have traveled to Syria to join the fighting. There have been official warnings that some have already come back to plot terrorist attacks inside Britain. The national threat level has been raised to "severe," indicating an attack is considered highly likely.

Police officers have been warned to be vigilant about their own safety. A fighter who returned from Syria was part of one British group accused of plotting a terror attack against police, and recent attacks in Canada and the United States against soldiers and police have made Britain wary.

Officials say the Portsmouth fighters, all of Bangladeshi origin, are just a drop in the bucket, with most of the Syria-bound jihadis coming from the metropolitan sprawls around London and Birmingham. But Portsmouth's problems are being replicated in dozens of similar small cities throughout Britain.

It's been known for months that four young Portsmouth men left together - they were photographed on CCTV traveling through the airport headed for Syria. But the recent deaths of two of the men, and the arrest of a third on terrorist charges after he returned to Britain, have unnerved the city.

"This has really rocked the Muslim community in Portsmouth to its core," said Donna Jones, leader of the city council. "They didn't see the signs coming."

CAGE research director, Asim Qureshi talks, during a press conference held by the CAGE human rights charity in London. A British-accented militant who has appeared in beheading videos released by the Islamic State group in Syria bears "striking similarities" to a man who grew up in London, a Muslim lobbying group said. Mohammed Emwazi has been identified by news organizations as the masked militant more commonly known as "Jihadi John." London-based CAGE, which works with Muslims in conflict with British intelligence services, said its research director, Asim Qureshi, saw strong similarities, but because of the hood worn by the militant, "there was no way he could be 100 percent certain", February 26, 2015. (AP Photo/Matt Dunham)

The group that has traveled to Syria has included those from families well-off and poor, she said. They ranged in age from 19 to 31.

Jones believes the urge to travel to Syria began with people feeling sympathy for Syrian civilians trapped in the civil war, then evolved into something more sinister.

The mother of 19-year-old Muhammad Mehdi Hassan had told British reporters that he wanted to come home. She said she went to the Turkish border to help him get out of Syria. Although she made it to within a few miles (kilometers) of her son, she said he could not break free and get to the border. British officials believe

Islamic State commanders will not allow disillusioned fighters to leave - and it is clear they would face arrest upon returning to Britain.

Hassan was killed in October in fighting in the border city of Kobani. His family learned about his death when a photo of his body was posted on Twitter.

His family released a statement after his death characterizing Hassan as "a loving boy with a good heart wishing to help Syrians. ... This is a tragedy and a lesson."

To prevent others from going, police are reaching out to the Muslim community so that parents who notice changes in their children's behavior will be willing to contact the authorities, said Chief Inspector Alison Heydari.

"We want people who identify problems to feel they can trust police and make referrals to us," she said. There have been some referrals, she said, declining to provide details.

In the past, Britain has seen several notorious preachers with known terrorist links use local mosques to kindle interest in jihad. That doesn't seem to be the case in Portsmouth. No authorities accuse leaders of the Jami Mosque of urging Muslims to embrace violence.

Instead, they blame incendiary material easily found online.

"There is a lot being done on the Internet," Jones said. "I think there's targeting being done, aimed at young Muslim men. I think social media is very powerful now."

She said it was likely that the late Iftekar Jaman, the first Portsmouth man to travel to Syria for jihad, found the support he needed online and then recruited others from Portsmouth.

Security officials agree that British mosques have in the last decade played a declining role in radicalization. At the same time, a generation gap has opened - with younger, better-educated Muslims using the Internet to pick up and exchange information.

Haque said he knows many of the parents whose sons went to fight - and that they were shocked by their sons' abrupt departures. The parents had no idea their sons were interested in jihad and in retrospect believe they got the idea from Twitter, Facebook, YouTube and other Internet-based forms of communication.

"None of the older generation knew anything about it," Haque said. "No parents can have control over this. They don't know what their children are up to."

TONE SOUNDS MUCH LIKE NPR
Paris, France, Monday, June 1, 2015

After a selection of tunes, the presenter with an American accent offers "a glimpse at our main headlines." IS militants have just seized three Iraqi cities. A bomb blows up a factory, killing everyone inside. Militants destroy four enemy Hummers and an armored vehicle.

The newscast's tone sounds much like National Public Radio in the United States. But this is Al-Bayan, the Islamic State radio targeting European recruits - touting recent triumphs in the campaign to carve out a Caliphate.

All news is good news for Al-Bayan's "soldiers of the Caliphate." In this narrative, the enemy always flees in disgrace or is killed. The broadcasts end with a swell of music and a gentle English message: "We thank our listeners for tuning in."

The tension between the smooth, Western-style production and the extremist content shows how far the hardcore Islamic propaganda machine has come since 2012, when an aging Frenchman posed in front of a black-and-white jihadi flag and threatened France in the name of al-Qaida in the Islamic Maghreb. The footage was grainy, with minimal production values, and released on a relatively obscure regional website. By contrast, Al-Bayan reaches thousands of listeners every day via links shared on social networks, helping to swell the ranks of Westerners - projected this year to reach a total of up to 10,000 - fighting for the Islamic State group in Syria and Iraq.

In the time it took to bring the Frenchman Gilles Le Guen to trial, his European successors in violent jihad have overturned the recruitment script in ways that might impress a New York PR agency.

Islamic State videos come with thrumming beats, handsome clear-eyed young men and editing techniques that call to mind tourism commercials or ads for the latest console game. A typical week of recruitment now includes multiple newscasts in three languages, except the "good news" is about suicide attacks instead of traffic reports and baseball scores. A polished video directed at French recruits shows trainees leaping through burning hoops and swinging across monkey bars over flames. Multilingual blog posts by jihadis urge people to follow them. And a metastasizing network of tweets spills forth from the smartphones of armchair cheerleaders.

Cameramen themselves are heroes in this information war: Media, an unnamed fighter says in a video dedicated to these PR muhajedeen, is "half of the battle, if not its majority."

A suicide bomber, with the Arabic bar below reading: "Urgent: The heroic martyr Abu Amer al-Najdi, the attacker of the (Shiite) temple in Qatif", which the Islamic State group's radio station claimed responsibility for, May 23, 2015. (AP Photo/Militant Website)

An April video calling for doctors to join IS shows physicians in immaculate scrubs, as well as clean and functioning medical equipment. It features a clean-shaven, blue-eyed Australian moving about in a pristine neo-natal ward, promising new recruits that they will be helping Muslims who suffer from "a lack of qualified medical care." The video has the feel of a daytime television public-service message.

In an exchange on jihadi radio station Ask.fm the same week, a person identifying himself as a British resident of Islamic State territories promised newcomers free medical school with minimal entry requirements. Meanwhile, in a series of tweets, another person purporting to be a Briton praises subsidized gas, free water and dental care superior to anything offered in the West.

"Naturally the arrogance will kick in & they would deny the truth and claim there (sic) way is better. Lol next time you pay your bill smile," the person said, according to a selection of tweets culled by the SITE Intelligence Group.

A handful of people show up repeatedly as key recruiters: a Glasgow woman who reportedly helps British girls reach Syria; a Dutch fighter who gives jihadi interviews and set up a Tumblr page; a blue-eyed Frenchman who appears in multiple videos calling on his countrymen to emigrate to IS territories.

When Le Guen was arrested in April 2013, France's defense minister said the government could "count on the fingers of one hand" those who, like him, wanted to fight alongside Islamic extremists. Now, the mass recruitment of Western Islamic radicals is considered one of the greatest security threats faced by Europe and the United States.

"They want Europeans in general. They want anyone to come, to fight, to create the Islamic state, to make the caliphate," said Sebastien Pietrasanta, a French lawmaker who is spearheading nascent efforts to de-radicalize young extremist recruits. "We estimate there could be 5,000 and within the year, there could be 10,000. ... We are facing not just a problem of security, but a problem of society."

And the group isn't just calling for weathered would-be fighters. As its new multimedia drive shows, anyone willing to help in the war zones of Syria and Iraq is welcome. One-way travel is encouraged, but not mandatory - at least, for men.

Anyone, from anywhere, can recruit for Islamic State. A March study by Brookings Institute researchers J.M. Berger and Jonathon Morgan found more than 46,000 active Twitter accounts supporting Islamic State in a two-month period. As soon as one account is shut down, more emerge.

Meanwhile, Western government warnings about the dangers of joining Islamic State have barely dented the rate of departures. Those who have lived unhappily under IS rarely offer a competing narrative, in mortal fear of retaliation. And Western nations are having a hard time combatting rhetoric that they - and the Western media that IS so successfully mimics - are untrustworthy.

Islamic State recruits skew young. In France, the West's largest source of extremists heading to Iraq and Syria, they average in their mid-20s, with female recruits tending to be even younger. Whatever they are looking for, Islamic State promises: Shariah law, a deeper purpose in life, a fight against a dictator, aid work, automatic weapons, pathological violence for those so inclined.

A poster with a picture of a late Jordanian Salafi Jihadi, who was killed by Syrian government forces while fighting alongside Jabhat al-Nusra, or al-Nusra Front, an al-Qaida affiliate in Syria, and Arabic that reads "the martyr Jihadi sheikh Osama Kreishan, Abu Abdullah, martyred in Syria Friday, January 3, 2014," is posted on the wall of his family house, in the city of Maan, Jordan, October 27, 2014. (AP Photo/Nasser Nasser)

The top U.S. military man in Europe attributes the success of Islamic State recruiting to its understanding of what many young people yearn for, as well as the group's ability to harness cutting-edge technology and personal connections. Western recruits tend to cluster, like the 20-odd young men from the small French town of Lunel who left in groups of two or three and rejoined each other in Syria; the three British schoolgirls who followed months after the departure of a friend; or the group of young Spaniards accused of plotting attacks at home when they realized they would be blocked from going to Syria.

"They are able to reach and find out what is important to these people, what motivates these people, and then they create an ability to fill that need, initially through the social media, Internet," Air Force General Philip Breedlove, NATO's supreme allied commander for Europe, said recently. "And then when they bring them on board, they continue to address these basic wants, of value, of a purpose - a sense of something as a part of a larger good. And whether it's right, wrong or indifferent, they are able to reach into these people and find that motivation."

Governments have failed at countering the tailor-made messages. John G. Horgan, of the University of Massachusetts' Center for Terrorism and Security Studies, thinks it's because Western intelligence agencies are looking at the caliber of recruits, instead of the sophisticated and enticing grooming process.

"It is phenomenally exciting for them to be part of this, this secret club," Horgan said. "And once that takes root ... that excitement completely outweighs anything we can do to try to counter it."

An e-book of travel advice feeds on the excitement, advising people to bring military-grade knives, a compass and solar chargers because "you will be minimizing wastage and polluting less." It recommends bringing an extra set of clothes for changing after the dash under barbed wire.

Few who have abandoned life under Islamic State are willing to talk about it, although security officials say about a third of European fighters have returned home. The group threatens traitors with death and has carried out that threat in Syria, if not in the West. But Peter Neumann of the International Centre for the Study of Radicalisation and Political Violence at Kings College London says their voices will ultimately be the most effective at dissuading more departures, if governments can ensure they face no risk.

"Right now it's really only Islamic State who is telling a story," he said. "To have a counter-story being told by a former fighter would be potentially very powerful."

There will be no counter-story from the young man from Belgium who joined Islamic State after becoming convinced that his Arab name torpedoed any future in his homeland.

The man's mother said she found him a few small jobs and tried to convince him that his place was in Belgium - "that he had a future ... that jihad was to have the courage to look every day for work." She spoke to The AP on condition of anonymity for fear of what might happen to her government job if it became known that she had raised an Islamic extremist.

The people the young man met hanging around Brussels-area mosques, coupled with the videos he saw online, had a more alluring pitch.

Mehdi "DJ Costa" Akkari, a Tunisian rapper in Tunis, Tunisia, looks at an image of his brother Youssef, who fought with extremists in Syria and was killed by a U.S. airstrike. While foreigners from across the world have joined the Islamic State militant group, some arrive in Iraq or Syria only to find day-to-day life much more austere and violent than they had expected, December 4, 2014. (AP Photo/Paul Schemm)

"They told him he could help people in Syria," the mother said. In a phone call home, he told her of his intention of building the caliphate and dying as a martyr. At age 19, Anis, also known as Abu Ibarhim al-Belgiki, was reported killed on the last day of February in the battle for Deir al-Zour airport in Syria.

His mother was told he was hit in the head by a bullet - and buried near the spot where he fell.

Chapter 7

CAPTIVE

Yazidi Kurdish women chant slogans during a protest against the Islamic State group's invasion of Sinjar city one year ago, in Dohuk, northern Iraq. Thousands of Yazidi Kurdish women and girls have been sold into sexual slavery and forced to marry Islamic State militants, according to Human Rights organizations, Yazidi activists and observers, August 3, 2015. (AP Photo/Seivan M. Salim)

'WHERE IS GOD?'
Dahuk, Iraq, Friday, October 3, 2014

One of the most haunting memories 70-year old Aishan Ali Dirbou has of her encounter with Islamic State militants who overran her hometown is feeling the ends of their AK-47 assault rifles dig into her side as she lay face down, pretending to be dead.

Today, the widow is one of tens of thousands of members of Iraq's Yazidi religious minority, who after fleeing the town of Sinjar last month, are now living in squalor in unsanitary shelters and camps, with little food or water and no medicine - uncertain what their future holds.

The Kurdish military says it is now on a push toward Sinjar, located in the desert of northwestern Iraq near the Syrian border, in an assault aimed at retaking the town from the extremists. The past week, Kurdish fighters retook three towns just north of Sinjar - Mahmoudiyah, the Rabia border cross and the town of Zumar - with the help of U.S.-led airstrikes.

The Yazidis now living in the Kurdish city of Dahuk are cautiously optimistic -wary after having already lost so much, but hopeful to return home and pick up the pieces.

An Iraqi internally displaced Yazidi boy, held by his mother, waits for a treatment at a clinic in the town of Khanke, outside Dahuk, 260 miles northwest of Baghdad, August 17, 2014. (AP Photo/Khalid Mohammed)

At the Badlees Primary School, nearly 250 Yazidis are crammed in, some of them 28 to a room. Many are growing desperate, with nothing but handouts to feed them, and the clothes on their backs to keep them warm as winter creeps closer. The Kurdish government has provided some aid in the way of foodstuffs and thin cushions to sleep on, but the central government in Baghdad has made no contact, the refugees said.

Three families gathered around a small pan of eggs, sharing a piece of bread among them. Outside, dozens of eggshells littered the ground alongside a tiny portable stove used to cook for all the residents. Outside, children fill up containers with water from a tank on the playground, but the water is not clean enough to drink. Inside, a woman washes children's clothes in a small muddy tub.

The rainy season has begun in this mountain city. Earlier this week, a few inches of rain flooded the school, packing the grounds where families sleep and children play with several inches of soggy mud.

They spoke of harrowing ordeals when the Islamic State group militants - who consider the Yazidis a heretical sect - stormed into Sinjar and nearby villages. The United Nations estimates that more than 1.8 million Iraqis were displaced this year as the militant group violently swept across western and northern Iraq.

Tens of thousands of Sinjar residents quickly fled into the nearby mountain range. Dirbou said she had no way out and no one to come to her rescue. When the gunmen swept by her home, Dirbou said she played dead. The gunmen prodded her with their rifles, then moved on.

For six days, she walked - and when she couldn't walk, she crawled - attempting to make her way to the Sinjar Mountains. When she was spotted by a few militant sympathizers, they took pity on her, giving her a piece of bread to hold her over. After 10 days on the mountain, she and others were rescued in an airlift and taken to Dahuk. There she was reunited with her daughters and their families - but many of her other relatives are missing, prolonging the ordeal.

"The fear has not stopped just because we ran from Daesh," she said, using the Islamic State group's Arabic acronym. "Sometimes I believe I was lucky to get away, but other times I feel it (would have been) better to die."

Other Yazidis in Dahuk recounted stories of babies and elderly relatives being shot by the militants.

"Where is God?" asked Amal, one of few Muslim Sinjaris staying at the school. She withheld her last name out of fear. "I am sure some of us will not survive to see Sinjar again."

Many of them are missing loved ones and say the militants captured their sisters and daughters, taking them to unknown locations, for unknown reasons.

Iraqis from the Yazidi minority near their makeshift homes on Mount Sinjar in northern Iraq 250 miles northwest of Baghdad. Thousands of Yazidis fled up the rocky slopes of Mount Sinjar to escape the Islamic State group during its rampage across northern Iraq last summer. Many still remain on the mountain despite gains by the Kurdish Peshmerga forces against the militant group, January 12, 2015. (AP Photo/Seivan Selim)

"My father and mother were killed," said Renaz Ravo, 16, a Yazidi who said her sister was taken captive by the militants along with dozens of other women. "I wish I could go look for her."

At least a dozen families who spoke to The Associated Press reported missing female relatives, many of them saying the last word they had last received from the missing girls is that they were in the town of Tal Afar, one of the militant's biggest strongholds in Iraq. They were eager to provide names and offer any information about their whereabouts in the hope they can be found.

In August, officials with the Iraqi Human Rights Ministry said that hundreds of Yazidi women and girls had been taken by the Islamic State militants. Yazidi lawmaker Vian Dakheel made an emotional plea in parliament to save the women, saying they're being used by the jihadi fighters as slaves.

At the Badlees School, the families all asked eagerly for news about the Kurdish forces' offensive toward Sinjar. Their hopes for its success were tempered.

When asked about the possibility of returning home, almost all gave a cautious reply - "Allah kareem," Arabic for "God is generous."

SOLD AS A SLAVE
Maqluba, Iraq, Saturday, October 11, 2014

The young Yazidi girl rocked apprehensively as she described the ordeal that took her from her family, snatched from her home by militants in Iraq, then sold as a slave in Syria before finally escaping to Turkey.

The 15-year-old is now with what is left of her family - two of her brothers and some more distant relatives - living in a makeshift roadside shelter in this tiny village in northern Iraq, along with other families shattered by the onslaught from the Islamic State militant group.

Her two sisters remain in the militants' hands, and her father, other brothers and other male relatives have vanished, their fates unknown.

The girl was among hundreds of women and girls from the Yazidi religious minority captured by Islamic State fighters in early August when the militants overran her hometown of Sinjar in northwestern Iraq. Hundreds were killed in the attack, and tens of thousands fled for their lives, most to the Kurdish-held parts of northern Iraq.

Iraq's Human Rights Ministry said at the time that hundreds of women were abducted by the militants, who consider the Yazidis a heretical sect.

The Associated Press spoke to the girl and several other young women who escaped captivity by the Islamic State group. While specifics of their stories could not be independently confirmed, they reflected circumstances reported by the United Nations last month.

They each independently painted a similar picture of how the militants scattered them around the broad swath of territory controlled by the Islamic State group in Syria and Iraq and sold the girls to the group's foreign fighters or other supporters for "marriage."

For weeks after being snatched from Sinjar, the 15-year-old girl and two of her sisters were shifted from one place to another, she said. The AP does not identify victims of abuse, and the girl also did not want to be named for fear of reprisals against her relatives still being held by the militants.

As she told her story, the girl rubbed her hands and avoided eye contact. But she spoke decisively and clearly, never hesitating when asked questions. She asked her relatives to leave the room, saying she was more comfortable speaking alone.

A 15-year-old Yazidi girl captured by the Islamic State group and forcibly married to a militant in Syria sits on the floor of a one-room house she now shares with her family after escaping in early August, while speaking in an interview with The Associated Press in Maqluba, a hamlet near the Kurdish city of Dahuk, 260 miles northwest of Baghdad, October 8, 2014. (AP Photo/Dalton Bennett)

First, she said, she and other girls were taken to the nearby town of Tal Afar, where she was kept in the Badosh Prison. When U.S. airstrikes began around the town, the militants took her and many other girls with them to the Islamic State group's biggest stronghold, Mosul, in northern Iraq.

From the city of Mosul, she and her sisters were taken to the militants' de facto capital, the Syrian city of Raqqa. There they were held in a house with other abducted girls.

"They took girls to Syria to sell them," she said, her body shyly hunched over as she spoke. "I was sold in Syria. I stayed about five days with my two sisters, then one of my sisters was sold and taken (back) to Mosul, and I remained in Syria."

In Raqqa, she said, she was first married off to a Palestinian man. She claims she shot him, saying the Palestinian's Iraqi housekeeper who was in a dispute with the man helped her by giving her a gun. She fled, but she had nowhere to run. So she went to the only place she knew, she said - the house where she was first held with the other girls in Raqqa.

There, the militants did not recognize her and sold her off again - for $1,000 to a Saudi fighter, she said. The Saudi militant took her to a house where he lived with other fighters.

"He told me, 'I'm going to change your name to Abeer, so your mother doesn't recognize you,'" she said. "You'll become Muslim, then I will marry you. But I refused to become a Muslim and that's why I fled."

She said she saw the fighters at one time taking a powdered drug. So she poured it into tea she served to the Saudi and the other men, causing them to fall asleep. Then she fled the house.

She found a man who would drive her to Turkey to meet her brother. Her brother then borrowed $2,000 from friends to pay a smuggler to get them both back to Iraq. They ended up in Maqluba, a tiny roadside hamlet just outside the Kurdish city of Dahuk, where several other Yazidi families are staying.

The other women who spoke to The AP described difficult conditions, where the militant fighters would deprive them of enough food, water or even a place to sit. They all reported having seen dozens of other Yazidi women and children as young as 5-years old in captivity, and they all said that they have relatives who are still missing.

Amsha Ali, a 19-year-old, said she was taken from Sinjar to Mosul. Ali was around six months pregnant at the time. The last she saw of her husband and other men in her family as she was being dragged off, was the scene of the militants forcing them to lie on the ground, apparently to shoot them. Ali agreed to be identified, saying she wanted the ordeals of the women to be known.

In Mosul, she said, she and other women were taken to a house full of Islamic State fighters to be married off. "Each of them took one of us for themselves," she said. She too was given to a fighter. She said she was never raped by the man - likely because of her pregnancy, she said - but she witnessed other girls being raped.

After several weeks, she was able to slip out of a bathroom window at night and escape. A Mosul resident who found her in the streets helped her get out of the city to nearby Kurdish territory on August 28, she said. She said she tried to convince other women to flee with her, but they were too afraid. "Because they were so terrified, they are left there and now I know nothing about them," she said.

Now Ali is with her father and a surviving sister living in an unfinished building in the town of Sharia, where some 5,000 Yazidi refugees live, also near Dahuk.

"The killing was not the hardest thing for me," she said of seeing fellow Yazidis slain in the assault on Sinjar. "Even though they forced my husband, brother-in-law and father-in-law on the ground to be murdered - it was painful - but marrying (the militant) was the worst. It was hardest thing for me."

HARD LINE INTERPRETATION OF ISLAM
Baghdad, Iraq, Sunday, October 12, 2014

Islamic State group militants captured, enslaved and sold Yazidi women and children, the latest issue of a magazine purportedly published by the extremists claimed Sunday, the group's first public confirmation of the allegations.

The claim came as Human Rights Watch said Sunday that hundreds of Yazidi men, women and children from Iraq are being held captive in makeshift detention facilities in Iraq and Syria by the group.

Tens of thousands of Yazidis fled into the Sinjar Mountains, many getting stranded there for weeks, after the militant onslaught on Sinjar in August, part of the Islamic State group's lightning advance across northern and western Iraq. Hundreds were killed in the attack, and tens of thousands fled for their lives, most to the Kurdish-held parts of northern Iraq.

Iraq's Human Rights Ministry said at the time that hundreds of women were abducted by the militants, who consider the Yazidis, a centuries-old religious minority, a heretical sect. Some also alleged the Islamic State group enslaved and sold Yazidi women and children, though the group itself did not comment on it.

The issue of Dabiq magazine released Sunday stated that "the enslaved Yazidi families are now sold by the Islamic State soldiers." It added that "the Yazidi women and children were then divided according to the Shariah amongst the fighters of the Islamic State who participated in the Sinjar operations."

Life and Death in ISIS 123

Jinan Badel, the Yazidi author of the book "Jinan, Daesh's Slave" closes her eyes as she listens to speeches during the opening of an international conference on the religious and ethnic minorities being persecuted under the Islamic State group, in Paris, France. The conference includes high-level representatives from more than four dozen countries as well as international organizations and religious leaders, September 8, 2015. (AP Photo/Francois Mori)

An elderly Yazidi woman who was released by Islamic militants waits inside a bus before being driven to the Kurdish city of Dohuk, in Alton Kupri, outside Kirkuk, Iraq. The Islamic State group released about 200 Yazidis held for five months in Iraq, mostly elderly, infirm captives who likely slowed the extremists down, Kurdish military officials said. Almost all of the freed prisoners are in poor health and bore signs of abuse and neglect, January 18, 2015. (AP Photo/Bram Janssen)

Most of the Yazidis are now displaced in northern Iraq, many having lost loved ones in their flight to safety. Some say that their women and girls were snatched during the militant raid.

In one section of the magazine, a statement attributed to Mohammed al-Adnani, the spokesman for the Islamic State group, read: "We will conquer your Rome, break your crosses, and enslave your women," addressing those who do not subscribe to its hardline interpretation of Islam.

The release of the magazine came as New York-based Human Rights Watch said Yazidi men, women and children remain held by the group. Its report noted that the group "separated young women and teenage girls from their families and has forced some of them to marry its fighters."

One woman told Human Rights Watch that she saw Islamic State fighters buying girls, and a teenage girl said a fighter bought her for $1,000, the report said. The Associated Press independently has interviewed a number of Yazidi women and girls who escaped captivity and several claimed that they were sold to Islamic State fighters in Iraq and Syria.

HORRORS AT THE HANDS OF THE ISLAMIC STATE
Baghdad, Iraq, Tuesday, December 23, 2014

Women and girls from Iraq's Yazidi minority endured horrors at the hands of Islamic State group extremists after they were taken as slaves last summer, leaving them deeply traumatized, an international watchdog group said in a report issued on Tuesday.

The Amnesty International report based on interviews with over 40 former captives who were among hundreds of women and girls from the Yazidi religious minority captured by IS fighters in early August when the militants overran their hometown of Sinjar. Hundreds were killed in the attack, and tens of thousands were either stranded in nearby Mount Sinjar or fled mostly to the Kurdish-held parts of northern Iraq.

The London-based group said the captives, including girls aged 10-12, faced torture, rape, forced marriage and were "sold" or given as "gifts" to IS fighters or their supporters in militant-held areas in Iraq and Syria. Often, captives were forced to convert to Islam.

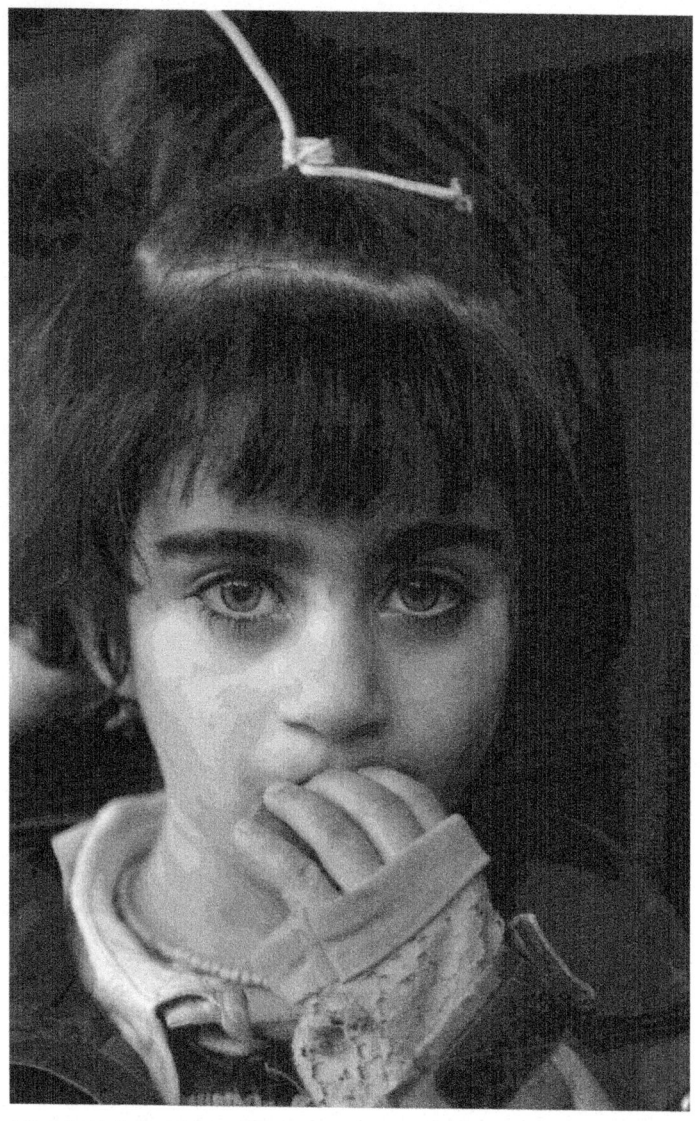

A Yazidi girl displaced by Islamic State group militants looks at a photographer in a partially constructed building serving as a home for several families in Dohuk, northern Iraq, December 10, 2014. (AP Photo/Seivan Selim)

"Hundreds of Yazidi women and girls have had their lives shattered by the horrors of sexual violence and sexual slavery in IS captivity," Amnesty's Senior Crisis Response Adviser Donatella Rovera said in a statement.

"Many of those held as sexual slaves are children - girls aged 14, 15 or even younger," Rovera added.

Fearful of rape, some captives committed suicide - like the 19-year old Jilan, according to her brother and one of the 20 girls who were with her.

"One day we were given clothes that looked like dance costumes and were told to bathe and wear those clothes," said the girl quoted in the report. "Jilan killed herself in the bathroom. She cut her wrists and hanged herself. She was very beautiful; I think she knew she was going to be taken away by a man and that is why she killed herself," added the girl, who was among those who later escaped.

It was unclear how many Yazidi women were abducted, but Iraq's Human Rights Ministry put the number in the "hundreds." Amnesty reports said the number is "possibly thousands."

An Iraqi Assyrian woman who fled from Mosul to Lebanon holds a placard depicting the map of Iraq and Syria, during a sit-in for abducted Christians in Syria and Iraq, at a church in Sabtiyesh area east Beirut, Lebanon, February 26, 2015. (AP Photo/Hussein Malla)

The Yazidis are a centuries-old religious minority viewed as apostates by extremists in Iraq. They have suffered religious persecution for generations because of their beliefs, which include some elements similar to Christianity, Judaism and other ancient religions. Many Muslims consider them devil worshippers, an accusation that Yazidis strongly dispute.

The June onslaught by IS stunned Iraqi security forces and the military, which melted away and withdrew as the extremists advanced, capturing key cities and towns in the country's north. The militants also targeted Iraq's indigenous religious minorities, including Christians and Yazidis, forcing tens of thousands from their homes.

Since then, the Islamic State has carved out a self-styled caliphate in the large area straddling the Iraqi-Syrian border that it now controls.

Alarmed with their advance, the United States launched airstrikes in early August on the militant-held areas in Iraq, in an effort to help the Iraqi forces repel the growing militant threat. Since then, some progress has been made on the ground by government forces, Kurdish fighters and Shiite militias.

Chapter 8

THE ALLURE OF THE ISLAMIC STATE

Islamic State militants pass by a convoy in Tel Abyad town, northeast Syria, May 4, 2015. (AP Photo/Militant Website)

JIHADS LEGIONNAIRES
Pankisi Gorge, Georgia, Thursday, May 21, 2015

One day this April, instead of coming home from school, two teenagers left their valley high in the Caucasus, and went off to war.

In Minneapolis, Minnesota, a 20-year-old stole her friend's passport to make the same hazardous journey.

From New Zealand, came a former security guard; from Canada, a hockey fan who loved to fish and hunt.

And there have been many, many more: between 16,000 and 17,000, according to one independent Western estimate, men and a small number of women from 90 countries or more who have streamed to Syria and Iraq to wage Muslim holy war for the Islamic State.

Abu Bakr Al-Baghdadi, the group's leader, has appealed to Muslims throughout the world to move to lands under its control - to fight, but also to work as administrators, doctors, judges, engineers and scholars, and to marry, put down roots and start families.

"Every person can contribute something to the Islamic State," a Canadian enlistee in Islamic State, Andre Poulin, says in a videotaped statement that has been used for online recruitment. "You can easily earn yourself a higher station with God almighty for the next life by sacrificing just a small bit of this worldly life."

The contingent of foreigners who have taken up arms on behalf of Islamic State during the past 3 1/2 years is more than twice as big as the French Foreign Legion. The conflict in Syria and Iraq has now drawn more volunteer fighters than past Islamist causes in Afghanistan and the former Yugoslavia - and an estimated eight out of 10 enlistees have joined Islamic State.

Mohamed Nidalha poses with a passport photo of his son Reda during an interview in Leiden, Netherlands. The 20-year-old Reda, who grew up liking girls and going to discos, suddenly changed, thanks to a toxic cocktail of online propaganda and covert contact with extremists in Belgium, one of Europe's hotspots for Islamic radicals, and eventually traveled to Syria, May 15, 2015. (AP Photo/Peter Dejong)

They have been there for defeats and victories. Following major losses in both Syria and Iraq, the fighters of Islamic State appear to have gotten a second wind in recent days, capturing Ramadi, capital of Iraq's largest Sunni province, and the ancient city of Palmyra, famous for its 2,000-year-old ruins.

There are battle-hardened Bosnians and Chechens, prized for their experience and elan under fire. There are religious zealots untested in combat but eager to die for their faith.

They include around 3,300 Western Europeans and 100 or so Americans, according to the International Center for the Study of Radicalization, a think tank at King's College London.

Ten to 15 percent of the enlistees are believed to have died in action. Hundreds of others have survived and gone home; their governments now worry about the consequences.

"We all share the concern that fighters will attempt to return to their home countries or regions, and look to participate in or support terrorism and the radicalization to violence," Nicholas J. Rasmussen, director of the U.S. government's National Counterterrorism Center, told a Senate hearing earlier this year.

Zarine Khan, right, and Shafi Khan, parents of Mohammed Hamzah Khan, attend a news conference after a hearing in their son's federal trial in Chicago. Zarine Khan, mother of the 19-year-old man facing a terrorist charge for trying to join Islamic State militants says the group is "brainwashing" youths via social media. And she declared, "Leave our children alone!", October 9, 2014. (AP Photo/Charles Rex Arbogast)

"Just like Osama bin Laden started his career in international terrorism as a foreign fighter in Afghanistan in the 1980s, the next generation of Osama bin Ladens are currently starting theirs in

Syria and Iraq," ICSR director Peter Neumann told a White House summit on combating extremist violence in February.

One problem in choking off the flow of recruits has been the variety of their profiles and motives.

Associated Press reporters on five continents tracked some of those who have left to join Islamic State, and found people born into the Islamic faith as well as converts, adventurers, educated professionals and people struggling to cope with disappointing lives.

"There is no typical profile," according to a study by German security authorities, obtained by AP.

The study reported that among people leaving that country for Syria out of "Islamic extremist motives," 65 percent were believed to have prior criminal records. They ranged in age between 15 and 63. Sixty-one percent were German-born, and there were nine men for every woman.

In contrast, John G. Horgan, a psychologist who directs the Center for Terrorism & Security Studies at the University of Massachusetts Lowell, found some common traits among American recruits or would-be recruits for jihad. Typically, he said, they are in their late teens or early 20s, though a few have been in their mid-30s.

The Islamic Center of Mississippi in Starkville, Mississippi, where 22-year-old Muhammad Dakhlalla was a member and his father, Oda H. Dakhlalla is the imam. Dakhlalla and 20-year-old Jaelyn Deishaun Young were charged in federal court with attempting to join the Islamic State and were ordered held without bail pending federal grand jury action on the charges, August 11, 2015. (AP Photo/Rogelio V. Solis)

"From a psychological perspective, many of them are at a stage in their lives where they are trying to find their place in the world - who they are, what their purpose is," Horgan said. "They certainly describe themselves as people who are struggling with conflict. They are trying to reconcile this dual identity of being a Muslim and being a Westerner, or being an American."

Some are driven by religious zeal to protect the caliphate, or Muslim theocracy, that the Islamic State has proclaimed in the one-third of Syrian and Iraqi territory now in its hands; others are thrilled by the chance to join what is tantamount to a secret and forbidden club.

Still others appear to enlist mainly because others do.

"What they have in common is that they are young, they are impressionable and they are hungry for excitement," Horgan said.

Once recruits arrive in areas held by Islamic State, they appear to receive only rudimentary military training - including how to load and fire a Kalashnikov assault rifle. Nonetheless, they have been involved in "some of the most violent forms of attacks" by the group, including suicide bombings and filmed beheadings of foreigners, said William Braniff, executive director for the National Consortium for the Study of Terrorism and Responses to Terrorism, a multidisciplinary research center headquartered at the University of Maryland.

Areeb Majeed, 23, from a suburb of Mumbai, India, joined Islamic State in May 2014 and fought for six months, killing up to 55 people and taking a gunshot to the chest.

But all was not heroics. He eventually called his parents from Turkey and asked to come home, according to Indian newspapers. Majeed's chief complaint, officials from India's National Investigation Agency were quoted as saying, was that the group didn't pay him, and made him clean toilets and haul water on the battlefield.

Often, though, the foreign combatants use social media to serve as "role models and facilitators for the next volunteers," Braniff said.

"Before I came here to Syria, I had money, I had a family, I had good friends, it wasn't like I was some anarchist or somebody who just wants to destroy the world, to kill everybody," said Poulin, the Canadian ISIS recruiter.

"Put God almighty before your family, put it before yourself, put it before everything. Put Allah before everything," the bearded and bespectacled transplant from Ontario urges in the video.

Poulin's jihad ended last August; he was reported killed during an assault on a government-controlled airfield in northern Syria.

But not, according to the Canadian Broadcasting Corp., before he had recruited five others from Toronto to come fight for the Islamic State.

DEATH ON A SYRIAN BATTLEFIELD
Rabat, Morocco, Thursday, May 21, 2015

Journalists and activists in Morocco during the heady days of the Arab Spring knew Anas Haloui, a slight, serious, wispy-bearded man in his 30s who would bombard them with emails about the plight of jailed Islamists.

Unlike many Salafis, as followers of his ultraconservative strand of Islam are known, he was eager to engage with people who didn't share his beliefs.

"He was a very nice guy, someone who was really open and trying to reach out to other people," recalled Brahim Ansari, Human Rights Watch's Morocco representative.

Anas Haloui speaks during a news conference of Salafis at the lawyers Club in Rabat, Morocco, February 2, 2012. (AP Photo/Rachid Tniouni)

But one day in December 2013, Haloui left behind his wife and children and quit Morocco to join a group linked to the Islamic State.

"I love my country with my last breath, but I was a victim of injustice, they put me in their cells and I don't need to remind you about the torture I went through," he said in a letter of farewell in which he condemned his treatment by the Moroccan government.

His older brother, Yusuf, remembers a different Anas - one who enjoyed singing. He recalls a cheerful boy in a family of eight kids growing up in the town of Tissa, just north of Fez in the foothills of the Rif mountains.

Anas majored in Islamic studies at Fez University in 1999, at a time of great intellectual ferment when Moroccan student life was dominated by Islamist groups. His brother says he never joined but took part in their activities, writing poetry for one group.

Everything changed after the 2003 Casablanca suicide bombings by young Islamic radicals that claimed 45 lives. Some 2,300 people were arrested, and Haloui was repeatedly questioned. He dropped out of school and returned home.

His efforts to distance himself from his student activism were in vain. He was arrested and convicted of forming an extremist group and spent three years in prison, during which he told his brother he was tortured by police and interrogated by American investigators.

In prison, he grew out his hair and beard and began wearing the traditional clothes associated with the Salafis, his brother said. When he got out in 2007, he was a changed man.

"He stopped singing after prison," said Yusuf. "It was like he was imprisoned by this Salafi idea."

But the 2011 Arab Spring demonstrations in the region inspired him. In Morocco, the February 20 Movement took to the streets to demand an end to corruption and abuse of power. Haloui joined the protests with secular activists. With other Salafis, who normally avoid all forms of activism or politics, he started an organization dedicated to freeing Islamist prisoners who he believed were being held unfairly.

Morocco got a new constitution promising greater freedoms. But the police soon returned to their old habits. One day men in plainclothes picked up Haloui's fiancee, slapped her around and warned her against marrying him.

Syrian President Bashar Assad in Tehran, Iran, August 19, 2009. (AP Photo/Vahid Salemi)

"After this his personality changed," said his brother. "His dreams were shattered."

Haloui's attention turned to the bloodshed in Syria, and the daily stories of civilians killed by the regime of President Bashar al-Assad.

"We know it is a war of extermination and that the only way to stop them from harming the innocents is through arms, God may one day ask us where we were during the Syrian events," he said in his goodbye letter, in which he expressed anguish over leaving behind his new wife and children.

From Syria, Haloui wrote that he was helping doctors treat the wounded. Four months later, in April 2013, his family learned through Facebook that he had died on a Syrian battlefield.

LOOKING FOR PARADISE
Minneapolis, Thursday, May 21, 2015

Abdifatah Ahmed struggled for years to make ends meet.

After losing his $15-an-hour job fueling airliners in Minneapolis, the Somali-American father of nine survived on low-wage jobs and public assistance. He complained about working hard, but never having enough money. His circumstances worsened when he was ordered to pay more than $700 a month to support three of his children - including one less than a year old.

Months later, he surfaced in Syria, where he went to fight for the Islamic State.

"I think since he lost his job, he was maybe never normal after that," sister Muna Ahmed told the AP last fall.

"It's unbelievable," his friend, Farhan Hussein, said recently. "Where did this disease come from?"

Hussein said his friend seemed confused about life, and sometimes felt stressed out by the women with whom he had children: Minnesota court papers show at times he was paying child support to two ex-wives for five of his kids, as well as support for a sixth whose mother is not identified. He wasn't the type to go to mosque or pray every day - instead, he went clubbing and even drank alcohol, Hussein said.

Abdifatah Ahmed after he was arrested for fleeing police in central Minnesota, 2003. (Benton County Sheriff's Department via AP)

When he felt troubled, Ahmed might turn to his religion for a week or so at a time. But once the blues passed, he would be back to his old self - flirting with women, dressing sharply, listening to rap music, shooting hoops and lifting weights at a local gym, Hussein said.

He dipped sporadically into political discussions, speaking about the Palestinians, the civil war in Libya and conditions in the Ogaden region of Ethiopia where many Somalis live. But the continued atrocities against Syrian civilians committed by the Assad regime apparently made a deeper impression.

On December 3, 2013, a post on his Facebook account showed pictures of mutilated kids: "Look what is happening in syria. Where is the UN when u need them. This is worse than libya you get it?"

A month later, it appears, Ahmed was in Syria himself.

"A muslim has to stand up for was right. ... I give up this worldly life for allah and to save the ummah (community of believers) if that makes terrorist am happy with it," he wrote in a January 3, 2014 post.

Another post that same day contains a photo of him holding a rifle in one hand, and a book that may be the Quran in the other.

Alarmed, Hussein messaged Ahmed, urging him to come home. After ignoring his friend for months, Ahmed replied that "we've got to fight" for the caliphate.

Ahmed's last Facebook posts, including one that says "having fun in jihad," are dated last July 25.

The next month, a member of Ahmed's family received a picture that appeared to show him dead, with a gunshot wound to the head. The State Department is working to verify reports of Ahmed's death, but Hussein identified the person in the photo as his friend, who would have been 34 according to court records.

Family and friends interviewed by the AP said they don't know what motivated Ahmed to go to Syria. Hussein said he may have been trying to escape financial troubles and the stress of being pulled in different directions by the women in his life.

"That's the only thing I could think of that would (mess) his life up, and make him lose his hope," Hussein said.

He added: "He was looking for paradise."

SPECIALLY DESIGNATED GLOBAL TERRORIST
Birkiani, Georgia, Thursday, May 21, 2015

In the summer of 2012, a former Georgian Army corporal who had served prison time for illegal possession of ammunition burned his photo albums and quit his native village.

Tarkhan Batirashvili had wanted to become a policeman, but couldn't get hired. Now, this offspring of a Christian father and a Muslim mother was about to start a new chapter in his military career - one in which he would be credited with some of Islamic State's most stunning battlefield victories and rise to senior rank.

Last September, the U.S. Treasury Department placed Batirashvili - who now calls himself Omar al Shishani and is believed by some to be Islamic State's chief of military operations - on its list of "specially designated global terrorists." But to some in the Pankisi, the mountainous region of northeastern Georgia where he was born in 1986, the ginger-bearded commander is a hero and a role model.

To follow the path he blazed, as many as 200 of his young countrymen have left their villages.

Batirashvili's father Temur is aghast.

"It's monstrous what's going on in the valley, that they are deceiving these kids and they're leaving to fight in a foreign land," the 72-year-old man told visitors to his one-story stone house in the hamlet of Birkiani. "My son should not be in Syria."

The Pankisi is home to an estimated 5,000-7,000 descendants of Muslim Chechens who settled here in the 19th century. In the village of Omalo, locals say, a green-tile roofed building is used by preachers from the Wahhabi branch of Sunni Islam to enlist volunteers for jihad.

Residents say the recruiters promise money and provide ground transportation to Tbilisi airport more than 120 miles (200 km) away, as well as prepaid plane tickets to Turkey.

"They are selling our children," said Shariat Tsintsalashvili. "They earn dollars from it, drive around in expensive four-wheel drive vehicles. It's a total mafia."

On April 2, her 16-year-old grandson Muslim Kushtanashvili and schoolmate Ramzan Bagakashvili, 18, joined the valley's recruits to Islamic State. That Thursday, the teens left as usual for their school in Omalo, next door to the building used by the Wahhabis. They never came home.

Temur Batirashvili, the father of Tarkhan Batirashvili, aka Omar al Shishani, speaks to The Associated Press at his house in the village of Duisi, April 8, 2015. (AP Photo/Shakh Aivazov)

Muslim called friends later to say he was in Turkey. Then word came back the 10th grader had crossed into Syria.

A legal minor, Muslim also had no passport, so his family can't understand why Georgian border guards let him fly out of the country. Interior Minister Vakhtang Gomelauri has vowed an investigation and punishment for those responsible, but Muslim's family suspect authorities are protecting the recruiters.

Bagakashvili's mother agrees.

"Here they are stirring up things, recruiting youths," Tina Alkhanashvili said. "You can't get authorities to watch them."

Within weeks, Georgian officials reported three more boys from the valley had disappeared.

VOLUNTEER FOR MARTYRDOM OPERATIONS
Amman, Jordan, Sunday, October 4, 2015

A Jordanian parliament member said he learned from Islamic State-linked media that his son carried out a suicide attack in Iraq, three months after dropping out of medical school and joining the extremist group.

The case highlights the continued grassroots appeal of IS ideas in the region, including in staunchly pro-Western Jordan, a partner in the U.S.-led military campaign against the group. IS militants have seized large parts of Syria and Iraq, both neighbors of Jordan.

"My son had everything, a family, money, and studying medicine, but he was controlled by terrible thoughts," the legislator, Mazen Dalaeen told The Associated Press. "He was deceived and tricked by Islamic State. Islamic State is in every home through TVs and the Internet."

On Sunday, the family observed the last day of the traditional three-day mourning for 23-year-old Mohammed Dalaeen. The family is from the town of Ai in southern Jordan that was also home to a Jordanian fighter pilot who was captured by IS late last year and burned alive in a cage by the militants.

The legislator said in the mourning tent that his son had changed rapidly in a short period and that at the beginning of the year he had taken part in a solidarity march for the pilot.

Jordanian parliament member Mazen Dalaeen speaks in the condolence house set up for the traditional three-day mourning period for his 23-year-old son, Mohammed Dalaeen, in Amman, Jordan. Dalaeen said he learned from Islamic State-linked media that his son carried out a suicide attack in Iraq, three months after dropping out of medical school and joining the extremist group, October 4, 2015. (AP Photo/Raad Adayleh)

Dalaeen said he learned of the death of his son last week from IS-linked media and a TV station in Iraq's Anbar province. One of the sites, Dabiq, said suicide attackers drove three car bombs into

Iraqi army barracks on the northern outskirts of Ramadi, the capital of Anbar.

Dalaeen said he recognized his son in one of the photos of the purported suicide attackers posted on the IS sites, under the nom de guerre "Abu Baraa, the Jordanian."

The legislator said he last saw Mohammed in Ukraine in June and stayed with him and his Ukrainian wife, a convert to Islam, for a week. Mohammed was a third-year medical student.

"I noticed that his behavior had changed completely," Dalaeen said in a phone interview Saturday. "He had become isolated" and had grown a large beard.

Dalaeen said he told his son in a heated argument that he would cut ties with him if he didn't drop his support for the extremists. The next day, Mohammed left for Turkey without telling his father.

Mohammed Dalaeen, a son of Jordanian parliament member Mazen Dalaeen, October 4, 2015. (AP Photo/Militant Website)

On August 20, Mohammed informed his father through Facebook that it would be their last contact. He wrote that he had completed his Islamic studies and would head into battle as a volunteer for "martyrdom operations," Dalaeen said.

An estimated 2,000 Jordanians are fighting in the ranks of IS and its militant rival from the al-Qaida network, the Syria-based Nusra Front, said Hassan Abu Haniyeh, an expert on extremist groups. He said about 350 Jordanians have been killed in fighting in the two countries.

This includes Omran al-Abadi, the son of Jordanian parliament member Mohammed al-Abadi.

Omran, an Egyptian-trained physician, joined the Nusra Front in Syria and was killed in January in a clash with the Syrian army. The legislator said Sunday that he did not hold the traditional mourning ceremony because he did not want to validate his son's actions.

"Those who fight in the ranks of such extremists mustn't be mourned, even by those closest to them," he said of his son's death.

Chapter 9

WOMEN OF THE ISLAMIC STATE

Asiya Ummi Abdullah, a 24-year-old Muslim convert who took her child to the territory controlled by the Islamic State, September 19, 2014. (AP Photo/Emrah Gurel)

'FALSE HEAVEN'
Istanbul, Wednesday, September 24, 2014

The Islamic State group is run by religious zealots and marked by war, mass killings, crucifixions and beheadings.

But for a growing number of fundamentalist Muslim families, the group's territory is home.

"Who says children here are unhappy?" said Asiya Ummi Abdullah, a 24-year-old Muslim convert who traveled to the group's realm with her infant son last month. She said that living under Shariah, the Islamic legal code, means the boy's spiritual life is secure.

"He will know God and live under his rules," she said.

Ummi Adullah's story, told to The Associated Press in a series of messages exchanged via Facebook, illustrates how, despite the extreme violence which the radical group broadcasts to the world, the territory it controls has turned into a magnet for devout families, many of them Turkish, who have made their way there with children in tow.

Ummi Abduallah said her move to the militant group's realm was in part to shield her 3-year-old from the sex, crime, drugs and alcohol that she sees as rampant in largely secular Turkey.

"The children of that country see all this and become either murderers or delinquents or homosexuals or thieves," she wrote.

The Islamic State group, the self-styled caliphate straddling Iraq and Syria, appears eager to attract families. One recent promotional video shows a montage of Muslim fighters from around the world cuddling their children in Raqqa against the backdrop of an amusement park where kids run and play.

A man, identified in the footage as an American named Abu Abdurahman al-Trinidadi, holds an infant who has a toy machine gun strapped to his back.

"Look at all the little children," al-Trinidadi says. "They're having fun."

It may promote itself as a family-friendly place, but the Islamic State group's bloody campaign for control of Syria and Iraq has uprooted hundreds of thousands of people in a wave of destruction that involves gruesome punishments and spectacular acts of cultural vandalism.

None of that matters to Ummi Abdullah.

"The blood and goods of infidels are halal," she said, meaning she believes that Islam sanctions the killing of unbelievers.

Ummi Abdullah's story has already made waves in Turkey, where her disappearance became front-page news after her ex-husband, a 44-year-old car salesman named Sahin Aktan, went to the press in an effort to find their child.

Many others in Turkey have carted away family to the Islamic State group under far less public scrutiny and in much greater numbers. In one incident earlier this month, more than 50 families from various parts of Turkey slipped across the border to live under the Islamic State group, according to opposition legislator Atilla Kart.

Kart's figure appears high, but his account is backed by a villager from Cumra, in central Turkey, who told AP that his son and his daughter-in-law are among the massive group. The villager spoke on condition of anonymity, saying he is terrified of reprisals.

Sahin Aktan shows a photo of his son Destan as he speaks during an interview at his lawyer's office in Istanbul, Turkey. Aktan, 44, is the ex-husband of Asiya Ummi Abdullah, a 24-year-old Muslim convert who took their child to the territory controlled by Islamic State. Her experience illustrates the puritanical pull of the Islamic State group. It also shows how, even in Turkey - one of the most modern and prosperous of the Muslim countries - entire families are dropping everything to find salvation in what one academic describes as a "false heaven", September 19, 2014. (AP Photo/Emrah Gurel)

The movement of foreign fighters to the Islamic State group - largely consisting of alienated, angry or simply war-hungry young Muslims - has been covered extensively. The arrival of entire families, many but not all of them Turkish, has received less attention.

"It's about fundamentalism," said Han, a professor of international relations at Istanbul's Kadir Has University. The Islamic State group's uncompromising interpretation of Islam promises parents the opportunity to raise their children free from any secular influence.

"It's a confined and trustable environment for living out your religion," Han said. "It kind of becomes a false heaven."

Ummi Abdullah's journey to radical Islam was born of loneliness and resentment. Born Svetlana Hasanova, she converted to Islam after marrying Aktan six years ago. The pair met in Turkey when Hasanova, still a teenager, came to Istanbul with her mother to buy textiles.

Aktan, speaking from his lawyer's office in Istanbul, said the relationship worked at first.

"Before we were married we were swimming in the sea, in the pool, and in the evening we would sit down and eat fish and drink wine. That's how it was," he said, holding a photograph of the two of them, both looking radiant in a well-manicured garden. "But after the kid was born, little by little she started interpreting Islam in her own way."

Aktan said his wife became increasingly devout, covering her hair and praying frequently, often needling him to join in. He refused.

"Thank God, I'm a Muslim," he said. "But I'm not the kind of person who can pray five times a day."

Asked why she became engrossed in religion, Aktan acknowledged that his wife was lonely. But in Facebook messages to the AP, many typed out on a smartphone, Ummi Abdullah accused her husband of treating her "like a slave."

She alleged that Aktan pressured her to abort their child and said she felt isolated in Istanbul. "I had no friends," she said. "I was constantly belittled by him and his family. I was nobody in their eyes."

Aktan acknowledged initially asking his wife to terminate her pregnancy, saying it was too early in the marriage to have children. But when she insisted on carrying the pregnancy to term, Aktan said he accepted her decision and loved the boy.

Meanwhile Aktan's wife was finding the companionship she yearned for online, chatting with jihadists and filling her Facebook page with religious exhortations and attacks on gays. In June, she and Aktan divorced. The next month, a day before her ex-husband was due to pick up their son for vacation, she left with the boy for Gaziantep, a Turkish town near the Syrian border. Aktan, who had been eavesdropping on her social media activity, alerted the authorities, but the pair managed to slip across.

It isn't clear how many families have followed Ummi Abdullah's path, although anecdotal evidence suggests a powerful flow from Turkey into Syria. In Dilovasi, a heavily industrial town of 42,000 about halfway between Istanbul and the port city of Izmit, at least four people - including a pair of brothers - recently left for

Syria, three local officials told AP. The officials, who spoke on condition of anonymity because they were not allowed to talk to the media, said that dozens of people from surrounding towns were believed to have left as well.

Aktan says he is in touch with other families in similar circumstances. He cited one case in the Turkish capital, Ankara, where 15 members of the same extended family had left for Syria "as if they're going on vacation."

Sahin Aktan shows a photo with his ex-wife Asiya Ummi Abdullah, September 19, 2014. (AP Photo/Emrah Gurel)

Even with U.S. bombs now falling on Raqqa, Ummi Abdullah says she has no second thoughts. "I only fear God," she wrote.

For Aktan, who says he hasn't seen his son since his ex-wife took the boy, her decision is a selfish form of fanaticism.

"If you want to die, you can do so," he said. "But you don't have the right to bring the kid with you.

"No one can give you this right."

Hours after the AP first published this story, Ummi Abdullah's Facebook account disappeared. Her messages to the AP were also removed, replaced with a message from Facebook saying they were "identified as abusive or marked as spam."

Facebook did not immediately return a message seeking comment.

LURED BY THE ISLAMIC STATE
Washington, D. C., Tuesday, December 16, 2014

As it looks to expand its territorial base across broad swaths of Iraq and Syria, the Islamic State group is recruiting for more than just fighters.

The extremist organization also has been targeting its sophisticated propaganda to entice potential wives and professionals such as doctors, accountants and engineers in its efforts to build a new society.

Among those it has lured were three teenage girls from Colorado, who set out for Syria this fall after swapping Twitter messages about marriage and religion with IS recruiters, and a young woman who sought to fight there - or failing that, to use her nursing skills. It's a diverse pool of recruits whose motives perplex Western governments seeking to combat the flow.

The group "is issuing a bit of a siren song through social media, trying to attract people to their so-called caliphate," FBI Director James Comey told reporters. "And among the people they're trying to attract are young women to be brides for these jihadis."

The group conscripts children for battle, recruits Westerners for acts of jihad and releases videotapes of beheadings. But it also uses propaganda with a humanitarian appeal, such as photos of bombed-out Syrian villages coupled with pleas for help. Video images of smiling children being given treats and enjoying stuffed animals paint a family-friendly portrait that suggests roles within the proto-state for wives and mothers.

Even as they preach violence, "they'll do the warm and fuzzy ... the gun in one hand and the kitten in the other," said Assistant Attorney General John Carlin, head of the Justice Department's national security division.

"They're seducing them with promises about how wonderful it will be," said Mia Bloom, a professor of security studies at the University of Massachusetts Lowell. "They promise a sense of adventure, that their worries will be addressed."

Apartment complex in Aurora, Colorado, which police say is the home of one of the three teenage girls who, according to U.S. authorities, were en route to join the Islamic State group in Syria when they were stopped at an airport in Germany, October 22, 2014. (AP Photo/Brennan Linsley)

Justice Department officials say people aiding the Islamic State understand what they're getting into and risk prosecution, whether or not they venture to Syria and even if they don't plan to take up arms themselves. Prosecutors have criminally charged more than 15 people in connection with supporting Islamic militant groups.

A Rochester, New York, food store owner stands accused of trying to arrange for others to travel to Syria and of plotting to kill members of the U.S. military. An Illinois man, allegedly determined to join militants, left behind a letter saying he was disgusted by Western society. And prosecutors say a North Carolina man asked Allah online for martyrdom.

Most charges are brought under a statute that makes it illegal to provide "material support" - including money, training or a false identity - to a designated terrorist group. Defense lawyers argued the law is overly broad and ensnares the misguided as often as it sweeps up the dangerous. Courts, however, have accepted an expansive interpretation of the law.

"We need to make clear that if you want to go over there and join a terrorist group, you're likely to end up instead in jail," Carlin said.

Justice Department officials say they're also trying strategies other than prosecution, including trying to identify potential recruits before they go.

FBI agents in Colorado met repeatedly with Shannon Conley, a 19-year-old nurse's aide who had converted to Islam, hoping to dissuade her from traveling to Syria to marry a militant suitor she met online. Agents suggested she try humanitarian work instead of jihad, but she told them that if she couldn't fight, she would use her skills as a nurse's aide to help militant fighters, according to court documents.

Conley pleaded guilty in September and faces sentencing next month. Her lawyer, Robert Pepin, has said she was "led terribly astray" while pursuing her religion and was "saved" by her arrest.

Perhaps no case better shows the penetration of the recruitment campaign than that of the three Colorado girls, all from East African immigrant families, who were radicalized online and headed for Syria in October.

A review of the girls' social media use, which included thousands of Twitter messages and postings on other sites, by the SITE Intelligence Group shows they were in contact with online jihadists from around the world and were deeply interested in marriage and the role of women. As recruiters interacted with the girls, their typical teenage banter about friends and school became replaced with discussions of religion, paradise and death, the review showed.

Six months before they went overseas, one girl wrote that she wanted to get married as soon as possible and her friends wished her well, telling her they hoped she got an "amazing husband because you do not deserve anything else!"

One female recruiter told prospects to expect to marry quickly and expect to live a domestic life, as it is "completely impossible for women to participate in battle," according to SITE. Women are expected to marry the fighters and bear their children, she explained. Another recruiter told a 16-year-old girl who inquired about joining that "everyone is welcome," according to the report.

U.S. officials say even comparatively benign motives for supporting the Islamic State are troubling. "I'm not sure we've seen someone who's gone over there who's not attracted to the jihadi cause," Carlin said.

MARTYRDOM, 'A GIRL CAN ONLY WISH'
Philadelphia, Friday, April 3, 2015

A woman was arrested Friday on charges she tried to join and martyr herself for the Islamic State group, a day after two women in New York were charged with plotting to wage jihad by building a bomb and using it for a Boston Marathon-type attack.

Philadelphia home of a woman who is accused of trying to join and martyr herself for the Islamic State group in Syria. Thirty-year-old Keonna Thomas appeared in federal court just hours after her arrest on a charge of attempting to provide material support and resources to a foreign terrorist organization. A prosecutor says a search warrant executed March 27 at Thomas' home prevented her from leaving the U.S. on a flight scheduled for March 29, April 3, 2015. (AP Photo/Matt Rourke)

Leonna Thomas, 30, was preparing to fly to Spain with hopes of reaching Syria to fight with the terror group, authorities said. Instead, she was arrested at her family's town house in a public housing development, which has three small U.S. flags adorning the porch.

Authorities said she communicated with an Islamic State group fighter in Syria who asked if she wanted to be part of a martyrdom operation. She told the fighter that the opportunity "would be amazing, ... a girl can only wish," according to the documents.

A federal magistrate ordered Thomas held pending a detention hearing Wednesday. Prosecutors will oppose bail.

Last month, Thomas bought a ticket to fly to Barcelona on March 29. She likely planned to take a bus to Istanbul and then reach Syria, according to an FBI affidavit filed in the case. Authorities put a stop to the trip when they raided her house March 27.

In court, Thomas wore a burqa as she acknowledged she understood the charge against her - attempting to provide material support and resources to a foreign terrorist organization. She was appointed a public defender, who did not comment on the charge.

Thomas appeared to show little emotion as she was led out of the house Friday morning in handcuffs, neighbor Ronni Patterson said. Patterson said she had seen investigators searching the home, where Thomas appeared to live with her mother and grandmother, a week ago.

The women in the New York case are accused of plotting to wage violent jihad by building a bomb and using it for an attack like the 2013 Boston Marathon bombings. They were ordered held without bail after a brief court appearance Thursday. The lawyer for one of them said his client will plead not guilty.

Mark Wilson, right, Colleen LaRose's defense attorney, speaks to members of the media outside the U.S. Courthouse in Philadelphia. LaRose, who authorities say dubbed herself "Jihad Jane" online, pleaded not guilty in federal court to a four-count indictment charging her in an overseas terrorist plot, March 18, 2010. (AP Photo/Matt Rourke)

Thomas is charged with attempting to provide material aid to terrorists, one of the same charges filed in 2010 against another

Pennsylvania woman, Colleen LaRose, known as Jihad Jane, and two co-defendants in a terror plot that prosecutors say also involved online messages and recruitment for overseas terror suspects.

"The incentive for terrorists is (also) ... to create fear, just by that ability to recruit within the U.S. They want to show everyone they have geographic reach and appeal," said defense lawyer Jeremy Ibrahim, a former Justice Department lawyer who represented LaRose's co-defendant Jamie Paulin-Ramirez, of Colorado. "But when you look at who actually responds to their calling, the women tend to be vulnerable."

Authorities have said foreign terrorists seek U.S. women because their Western looks and American passports make it easier for them to travel overseas.

Thomas' posts in support of the Islamic State group started in August 2013, when she reposted a Twitter photograph of a boy holding weapons, authorities said. She called herself Fatayat Al Khilafah and YoungLioness and tweeted posts such as "When you're a mujahid, your death becomes a wedding," according to the FBI affidavit filed in the case. A mujahid is one who engages in jihad.

She began trying to raise money for the cause online and told a Somalia-based jihadi fighter from Minnesota that she soon hoped to have enough money to travel, authorities said.

She applied for a passport in February and on March 26 bought a round-trip ticket to fly to Barcelona - a tourist destination that would not raise eyebrows, the FBI affidavit said.

LaRose got a 10-year term in January for agreeing to kill a Swedish artist who had offended Muslims, while Paulin-Ramirez, who married an Algerian terror suspect the day she met him in Ireland, is serving eight years.

An immigrant teen from Pakistan who met LaRose online when he was an honors student in suburban Baltimore was sentenced to five years in the case. All three agreed to cooperate with authorities, shaving years off their sentences.

AUSTRALIAN BRIDE
Canberra, Australia, Sunday, May 21, 2015

Quietly - almost secretly - Zehra Duman morphed from private school student to Islamic State bride and online recruiter for the movement. Her family did not see it coming.

So when the 21-year-old Turkish-Australian gave up her middle-class life in Melbourne, Australia's second largest city, for faraway Raqqa, the Islamic State movement's center in war-ravaged Syria, the people who knew her were astonished.

"We did not notice any extremist tendencies in her behavior," Saniye Coskundag, acting principal of Sirius College's Keysborough campus, told The Associated Press.

"She's been brainwashed, she wasn't like this three or four months ago," her father Davut Duman told Melbourne's Herald Sun newspaper in an article published December 28.

By then, Duman was wed to Islamic State soldier Mahmoud Abdullatif, 23, who reportedly left his own Melbourne home last year. The couple announced their wedding online on December 11, with a photograph of her dowry that included an assault rifle.

Now calling herself Zehra Abdullatif or Umm ("Mother") Abdullatif, the Muslim fighter's wife told her online followers her parents had no clue she would elope to the Islamic State.

"They were shocked, as I never have been public with my jihadi views. But also heartbroken, as my mum was very close to me ... and she knows she will never see me again," she said on her now suspended Ask.fm page, according to Radio Free Europe/Radio Liberty.

She has answered questions on social media for "wannabe jihadi brides," and urged both men and women sympathizers who do not come to the Middle East to wage war at home.

"Kill Kuffar (non-believers) in alleyways, stab them and poison them. Poison your teachers. Go to haram (prohibited) restaurants and poison the food in large quantities," she wrote on her Twitter account, which also has been suspended. The March 31 tweet was recorded by the Institute for Strategic Dialogue, a London-based think tank.

Australian security agencies have noticed an uptick in Australian women leaving for the Middle East to marry Islamic State fighters. Melanie Smith, a joint research fellow at the Institute for

Strategic Dialogue and ICSR who tracks more than 100 female migrants to Islamic State online, says they are prized additions to the self-styled caliphate.

"You cannot build a state without women, because there are no children," said Smith. Though Islamic State doesn't allow women a combat role, they are assured they will be honored as spouses of fighters and mothers of "cubs," the next generation of Muslim combatants.

It is not clear how or when Duman first met her husband, who she said died five weeks after their wedding. She said online she entered Syria alone in late November and was given a "wali," or guardian. She advised potential IS brides who follow her to travel with a "mahram," a male chaperone such as a father or brother.

Her father told the Herald Sun that he had not given up hope: "We're trying desperately, trying to bring our daughter home," he said.

But when asked on Twitter what she missed about Australia, Duman's reply on April 4 was simple and numeric: "0"

MANY REASONS FOR JOINING THE ISLAMIC STATE
London, Thursday, May 28, 2015

The notion that young women are traveling to Syria solely to become "jihadi brides" is simplistic and hinders efforts to prevent other girls from being radicalized, new research suggests.

Young women are joining the Islamic State group for many reasons, including anger over the perceived persecution of Muslims and the wish to belong to a sisterhood with similar beliefs, according to a report presented Thursday by the Institute for Strategic Dialogue and the International Center for the Study of Radicalization at King's College London.

Western societies must understand these varied motivations if they hope to prevent more women from joining the militants and potentially returning to their home nations to commit acts of terrorism, argue the report's authors, Erin Saltman and Melanie Smith. Thinking of them as all being brainwashed, groomed, innocent girls hinders understanding of the threat they pose.

"They're not being taken seriously," Smith said. "It's inherently dangerous to label people with the same brush."

International Centre for the Study of Radicalization, United Kingdom, Director Peter Neumann speaks at the Countering Violent Extremism (CVE) Summit at the State Department in Washington. The White House is conveying a three-day summit to bring together local, federal, and international leaders to discuss steps the US and its partners can take to develop community-oriented approaches to counter extremist ideologies that radicalize, recruit and incite to violence, February 19, 2015. (AP Photo/Pablo Martinez Monsivais)

The report was presented Thursday at a Jihadist Insurgency Conference at King's College. Saltman said women have always been involved in violent extremism, but that the number of women supporting Islamic State is "completely unprecedented."

"We see a real problem," she said, citing several factors for the increased numbers, including the direct call Islamic State is making for female volunteers, the fact that women are directly recruiting other women online, and the "very fluent, catchy, pop culture" approach the extremists use in their propaganda.

About 550 young women, some as young as 13, have already traveled to Islamic State-controlled territory, according to the report.

The researchers suggest that while the term jihadi bride may be catchy from a media point of view, the young women who are traveling to Syria see themselves as something more: pilgrims embarking on a mission to develop the region into an Islamic utopia.

Many would like to fight alongside male recruits, but the group's strict interpretation of Islam relegates them to domestic roles.

The primary responsibility for a woman in Islamic State-controlled territory may be to be a good wife and a "mother to the next generation of jihadism," but the study concluded that women are playing a crucial propaganda role for the organization by using social media to bring in more recruits.

"The propaganda is dangerous," Smith said. "It draws vulnerable or 'at risk' individuals into extremist ideologies ... simplifying world conflicts into good versus evil which allows someone the opportunity of being the 'hero' - an empowering narrative for a disenfranchised, disengaged individual."

Young women are often vulnerable to this kind of rhetoric because they are questioning their identities as they grow into adults. Many of the young women observed said they felt socially and culturally isolated in secular Western society, and saw the region controlled by Islamic State as "a safe haven for those who wish to fully embrace and protect Islam," according to the report.

Attorney Hassan Shibly speaks to the media at a mosque on behalf of the parents of a 20-year-old Islamic State militant recruit in Hoover, Alabama. He confirmed the family's daughter fled a Birmingham suburb to join Islamic State militants in Syria after being recruited over the Internet. Shibly said the woman identified as Hoda left in November after being "brainwashed" for an undetermined length of time. He said the woman's actions go against family's wishes and against the teachings of Islam, April 20, 2015. (AP Photo/Brynn Anderson)

The authors combed the social media accounts of more than 100 female profiles across platforms such as Twitter, Facebook and Tumblr. To grow their sample, they used a "snowball" technique in which female Islamic state migrants were identified among networks of other Islamic State networks. Photos, online chats and other accounts helped place the women geographically in Syria or Iraq. Researchers say the women came from 15 countries and were largely operating in English.

They consistently talked about the camaraderie they experienced after moving to Islamic State territory, and often used social media to post images of veiled "sisters" posing together.

"This is often contrasted with discussions about the false feeling or surface-level relationships they iterate they previously held in the West," the authors said. "This search for meaning, sisterhood, and identity is a primary driving factor for many women to travel."

They are also searching for romance in the form of marriage.

"Online, images of a lion and lioness are shared frequently to symbolize this union," the report said. "This is symbolic of finding a brave and strong husband, but also propagandizes the notion that supporting a jihadist husband and taking on the ISIS ideology is an empowering role for females."

One woman identified only as Shams and who is a qualified doctor, found her husband through an arranged meeting. He proposed immediately. She posted an image of her wedding, which features the Islamic State flag in the background. Her bearded husband wears a tie. She wears a white burqa with only a slit for the eyes.

She captioned the picture: "Marriage in the land of Jihad: Till Martyrdom Do Us Part."

While they are enticed by romantic stories about groups of women eating by candlelight and bathing in the Euphrates, most of the young migrants quickly find that the reality of their lives belies the rhetoric.

While life in Syria is difficult, few women voice their grievances directly. Islamic State has relied on a decentralized network of "messengers" to proliferate its world vision, and the network snaps into action to quickly reprimand anyone who speaks out. The hashtag "#nobodycaresaboutthewidow," didn't last long.

But the women do warn those who may follow them that they should be ready to "be tested" by intermittent electricity, water shortages, bitter winters and the travails of life in a war zone. Health care is a particular concern, with one Western woman describing her experience of having a miscarriage in an Islamic State hospital because she couldn't communicate with the doctor.

"These anecdotes serve to disprove the idea of the well-integrated, utopian society that is so strongly emphasized by ISIS propaganda," researchers said.

Chapter 10

COMING HOME

Omar Mansour, 23, right, who briefly joined jihadists in Syria, and his brother Abdullah, 21, who was recruited to join al-Qaida in Yemen, sit at the family house during an interview with the Associated Press, in the city of Maan, Jordan. Now they are home, trying to live ordinary lives, but believe their hardline vision of Islam is gaining popularity, October 28, 2014. (AP Photo/Nasser Nasser)

HOME FROM JIHAD
Maan, Jordan, Saturday, December 6, 2014

The three young Jordanians didn't start out as extremists. They grew up in mainstream Muslim families. But they grew increasingly angry at what they felt were Western injustices against Muslims - and decided to join the jihad in Syria and Yemen.

Now they are home from war, trying to live ordinary lives, knowing they are under heavy surveillance by Jordanian security agencies. Two brothers, Omar and Abdullah Mansour, are back in their father's house. A third returnee found a part-time teaching job and plans to marry.

But they abide by their hardline vision of Islam and are confident it is gaining popularity.

The Islamic State group could one day rule the region, said the teacher, who spoke on condition of anonymity for fear of trouble with Jordanian authorities. Its radical fighters are the defenders of Sunni Muslims against rival Shiites and the West, he said.

"They broke the head of America," he said, sitting in Maan's Great Mosque after noon prayers one day in late October. "They have taken back the rights of the Sunni people."

The bearded man - who sported a black vest over a gray robe, typical attire for ultraconservatives known as Salafis - said he grew up in a middle class family that was not particularly devout.

He said he was first drawn to jihadi Salafis while studying business administration at Maan's university. At the time, he said, he was driven by anger over what he felt was oppression of Muslims by U.S. troops in Iraq and Afghanistan.

He slipped into Syria this year. While he wanted to join Islamic State fighters, he ended up with their rival, the Nusra Front, al-Qaida's branch in the country. He spent seven months with Nusra fighters in a three-bedroom house in a town in southern Syria.

He said he gave religion classes to Nusra fighters and sometimes to fighters from the Western-backed Free Syrian Army - "the ones sympathetic to Islam."

Omar Mansour was in seventh grade when he first heard jihadi preachers on the Internet.

"I would listen to sermons about the situation of the Muslim nation, how important jihad is for God," he said in the spacious living room of his father's home.

Mansour, 23, said he repeatedly tried to join the rebels fighting Syrian President Bashar Assad, but was sent back by Jordanian border guards.

He finally sneaked across the border in late 2013. Like the teacher, he had hoped to join the Islamic State fighters but ended up with the Nusra Front because they operate closer to the Jordanian border.

He said in hindsight, it was preferable. "The problem with Islamic State is that they have killed Muslims." But, he added, the

Islamic State group is becoming more popular than al-Qaida because of its territorial gains.

Mansour said he saw combat and returned to Jordan about two months later for the birth of his daughter, Samar. He was detained and questioned for six weeks, and eventually got a job with a phosphate company.

His father Mahmoud, 48, said he was proud of his son. "I welcomed it," he said of Omar's jihad days.

Omar Mansour, second left, and his brother Abdullah, right, pose for a photo with their brother Ahmed, 19, left and their father Mahmoud, 48, at the family house, in the city of Maan, Jordan, October 28, 2014. (AP Photo/Nasser Nasser)

Omar's younger brother, 21-year-old Abdullah, was in prison in Yemen at the time, the family said.

Abdullah said he had dropped out of the local university in 2012 and boarded a plane to Yemen to fight in the ranks of al-Qaida. But, he said, he was caught by Yemeni security forces on the first day and spent two years in prison. He was released in February.

The return hasn't been easy. Abdullah hasn't been able to find work because he can't get the required security clearance for a government job.

After returning to Jordan in July, the teacher was also detained and interrogated for two months, then had to sign a pledge he would not promote Islamic State ideas. He was also warned he would be under surveillance.

He is treading carefully. He wants to start a family, maybe get a master's degree, and doesn't want to get arrested again.

"The Jordanian government is vigilant, and I don't think the U.S. and Israel would let this country fall to IS."

But, he said, growing economic pressure "might lead the country to an explosion."

EXTREMISTS BIDING THEIR TIME
Maan, Jordan, Saturday, December 6, 2014

Local authorities quickly stripped away public signs of support for the Islamic State group in this desert town. Black flags have been removed from rooftops. Graffiti proclaiming the extremists' imminent victory have been whitewashed.

But supporters of the Middle East's most radical extremist group are only laying low after their surprise show of strength in protests last summer. Despite government efforts, support for the Islamic State group is growing in Maan and elsewhere in Jordan, one of the West's key allies in the region, say Islamic State activists, members of rival groups and experts on political Islam.

One of the leading Islamic State group activists in Maan said he and others are still working to build their base.

"In homes, at work, in mosques, in the streets, we reach out to people to call them to the real Islam," the 40-year-old blacksmith, Abu Abdullah, told The Associated Press. Like other Islamic State group supporters interviewed by the AP, he spoke on condition he be identified only by his nickname for fear of troubles with authorities.

Militants like Abu Abdullah talk confidently of eventually having enough numbers to make their takeover of Jordan inevitable.

That may be overconfidence. Hardcore supporters of the Islamic State group's self-proclaimed "caliphate" likely number in the thousands in a nation of 6.5 million. The government says the threat is overblown. But extremists do have momentum, attracting followers with promises of radical change and an ostensibly more just society at a time when many Jordanians can't find jobs, struggle with rising prices or feel abandoned by the pro-Western ruling elite.

Two Jordanian men walk past graffiti depicting the flag of the Islamic State group with Arabic that reads, "There is only one God and Muhammad is his prophet," in the city of Maan, Jordan. Black flags have been removed from rooftops. Graffiti proclaiming the extremists' imminent victory have been whitewashed. But supporters of the Middle East's most radical extremist group are only laying low, October 28, 2014. (AP Photo/Nasser Nasser)

The war in Syria gives them a cause and battlefield experience. Up to 2,000 Jordanians are fighting in rebel ranks in Syria and Iraq, most of them with extremist factions, and several hundred have been killed, according to Hassan Abu Haniyeh, an expert on Islamic movements, and Marwan Shehadeh, a scholar who was once part of the ultraconservative Salafi movement.

Over the summer, jihadi Salafi marches were held in Maan, Zarqa and several other cities, with protesters raising black banners and chanting slogans in support of the Islamic State group.

Given the poverty and anger at perceived government neglect, such protests could easily erupt again and spread, warned Maan's mayor, Majed al-Sharari.

"My expectation is that because of this pressure, there will be a huge explosion in Jordan," he said. "I don't expect 2015 to pass peacefully. The signs are there."

Jordan's King Abdullah II called the fight against the Islamic State group and extremists "a third world war by other means."

"This is our war. This is a war inside of Islam," he said in an interview with CBS News on Friday ahead of White House talks with President Barack Obama. "We have to own up it. We have to take the lead."

Support for the Islamic State group runs strongest among jihadi Salafis. The jihadi Salafi movement backs the waging of violence - holy war, as they portray it - to bring about rule by the strict version of Islamic Shariah law that they contend is the only acceptable interpretation.

Experts estimate that the number of Jordan's jihadi Salafis has doubled since the 2011 outbreak of the Arab Spring uprisings, to at least 9,000 hardcore members.

They are part of the broader movement of Salafis, who number in the tens of thousands around Jordan. The vast majority in the movement opposes the jihadi branch and says preaching, not violence, is the way to spread their vision of Islam.

While they used to be focused in a few towns, "now you find jihadists everywhere in the kingdom," said Abu Haniyeh. They have increasingly turned to support for the Islamic State group since Jordan became part of a U.S.-led coalition waging airstrikes against the group in Syria and Iraq, he said.

Ibrahim al-Hmeidi, 44, a school supervisor and a Muslim Brotherhood member, talks during an interview with the Associated Press at his book shop, in Maan, Jordan, October 27, 2014. (AP Photo/Nasser Nasser)

They are also drawing from the ranks of the Muslim Brotherhood, once the region's most influential political Islamic movement. In Maan, jihadi Salafis are surpassing the Brotherhood in membership, said Ibrahim al-Hmeidi, a local school supervisor.

"There is a tangible increase in the number of supporters in the street," said Morad Adeili, spokesman of the Jordan branch of the Brotherhood. "People lost hope, particularly the young, and they feel the Salafi ideology and enterprise will give them what they want."

Maan, a tribal town of 60,000 in the deserts of southern Jordan, embodies the challenges. Unemployment in the province was 15 percent in 2013, compared to 12.6 percent nationally. Unemployment among those in their 20s is believed to be close to 30 percent.

Maan "has been marginalized for a long time by successive governments and there is real economic suffering," said the mayor, al-Sharari. "All we hear are promises and talk, but no real steps."

Dozens of Maan residents have gone to Syria or Iraq to fight in jihadi groups and at least 18 have been killed, according to Abu Abdullah, the Islamic State activist.

The show of IS support in Maan erupted in late June and early July, as Islamic State leader Abu Bakr al-Baghdadi declared a caliphate in the territory his group controls in Iraq and Syria. Pro-IS banners were hung from a two-story bank building in Maan that had been torched by rioters in April. "The Islamic caliphate is scoring victories," read one sign.

The announcement had jihadi Salafis in Maan at the time buzzing with excitement.

"The caliphate has become a reality on the ground and it will come here, sooner or later," said Abu Mohammed, who volunteers at the Sabeel Center, a local charity run by Salafis.

Another volunteer, 30-year-old Abu Ramez, said he hoped a caliphate will bring social justice. "We have two classes, the large poor one and the small rich one. Therefore, people support IS."

By late October, the flags were gone and most of the slogans whitewashed, under orders from the mayor.

But Abu Abdullah is undiscouraged. He said he expects Jordan to come under the control of the Islamic State group soon, with or without a fight.

"We are waiting for this moment," he said, sporting an untrimmed black beard, black headscarf and robe ending above the ankle, typical garb for Salafis.

Salafis are deeply intertwined in the conservative town and with its tribes, which hold powerful influence.

On a recent morning, for example, Mohammed al-Shalabi, a leading jihadi Salafi preacher widely known as Abu Sayyaf, had a casual get-together with senior tribal members to socialize and chat about the upcoming wedding of Abu Sayyaf's eldest son. They met at a furniture store owned by the head of Abu Sayyaf's clan.

The town's hundreds of Salafis are embraced by other members of their tribes, said Fayez Bazaya, one of the tribal leaders who attended. "When they (Salafis) face a problem, of course the tribe stands against the outsider."

Since the summer, the government has been reining in the pro-Islamic State fringe.

More than 120 have been arrested for support of the group the past three months. At least 16 have been sentenced to prison, including a man sentenced last week to three years in prison for "spreading terrorist ideology" by posting pro-Islamic State slogans on the Internet.

In the tough new climate, the Brotherhood also appears to be a target. Its deputy leader in Jordan was detained last month amid allegations he had harmed Jordan's relations with a friendly nation, a spokesman for the group said.

Salafi cleric Mohammed al-Shalabi, 48, widely known as Abu Sayyaf, talks during an interview with the Associated Press at a furniture store, owned by the head of Abu Sayyaf's clan, in the city of Maan, Jordan, October 29, 2014. (AP Photo/Nasser Nasser)

The flow of volunteer fighters to Syria and Iraq has also slowed because of tighter border restrictions, said Abu Abdullah.

Government spokesman Mohammed al-Momani dismissed talk of a threat to Jordan's stability.

"There is a huge exaggeration on the phenomena of extremism in Jordan," he said. "We are talking about a small phenomenon that is under control."

He acknowledged economic problems in Maan and other provincial towns but said the "mass majority of Jordanians don't associate with fundamentalism as an ideology and with terrorism in general."

After the rapid Islamic State gains in Iraq over the summer, there has been speculation it might target Jordan next, either through cross-border attacks or by trying to destabilize it from within. But the group also must take into account the likely strong response the U.S. would marshal to protect its ally.

Shehadeh said that for now, IS supporters see Jordan as "a land of logistical support and preaching, and it is not the land of the fight yet."

Abu Sayyaf said it's not the time for the Salafis to make their move. "The Salafis can change the country when they have power," he said. "When they are weak, they cannot."

RECRUITS FROM THE WEST
Berlin, Wednesday, June 3, 2015

A group of Western mothers whose children have joined the Islamic State group and other extremists in Syria and Iraq appealed Wednesday for them to return home, quoting from the Quran.

In an open letter posted on social media websites, members of Mothers for Life called on their sons and daughters to recall that Islam requires them to honor their parents and spare them suffering.

"Even if you think death will give you that 'better' life, remember that even the Prophet Muhammad (peace and blessings be upon him) said: 'Paradise lies at the feet of your mother,'" the group said. "By leaving us against our will to give up your own life and take those of others, you have put our struggle, pain and honor under your feet and walked over it."

Members of the Minneapolis Somali community gather outside the United States Courthouse in Minneapolis where a federal judge ordered four Minnesota men accused of trying to travel to Syria to join the Islamic State group held pending trial, May 12, 2015. (AP Photo/Jim Mone)

Thousands of young Western men and women have joined the Islamic State group in recent years after being recruited by other extremists, often operating online.

Mothers for Life - which has Muslim and non-Muslim members from seven countries including Canada, France and the United States - said their decision to launch the appeal on social media is part of a conscious effort to publicly challenge those who have lured their children away.

"Social media right now seems to be their strength in recruiting our youth," said Canadian mother Chris Boudreau, whose son was killed in Syria last year. "We've got to fight fire with fire," she told The Associated Press in a telephone interview.

The group also wants to help other families struggling to bring their children home, and highlight the need for politicians and security officials to take the parents of foreign fighters seriously.

Mothers for Life is run by the German Institute on Radicalization and De-radicalization Studies (GIRDS) in Berlin. It has several Muslims among its dozen members and also sought advice from Islamic scholars to challenge the religious arguments put forward by extremists.

DE-RADICALIZING JIHADISTS
Riyadh, Saudi Arabia, Wednesday, June 24, 2015

For most of his 20s, all Badr al-Enezi could think about was becoming a jihadi fighter. After getting in touch with former Guantanamo Bay prisoners who had returned to militancy, he began plotting how to take up arms.

Instead, he was caught by Saudi authorities and spent six months in prison. His next six months in detention were far different: He dabbled with art therapy, played soccer and enjoyed perks like an Olympic-size pool and a sauna at a rehab center for convicted extremists.

Gourmet-style meals were prepared for him at the palm-tree-lined complex on the outskirts of the Saudi capital, Riyadh, and his laundry was taken care of. He was treated "like a brother," he says.

Equally important, he was challenged to think differently about Islam.

And now, after successfully completing the de-radicalization program and renouncing any notion of fighting abroad, he serves as a mentor for new entrants to the center, named after Saudi Arabia's powerful interior minister, Crown Prince Mohammed bin Nayef.

Former Islamic militant, 30-year-old Badr al-Enezi, enters a courtyard at the Mohammed bin Nayef Center for Advice, Counseling and Care, as the rehab center is formally known, in Riyadh, Saudi Arabia, April 26, 2015. (AP Photo/Hasan Jamali)

"What is the secret? It is that the ideas we carry cannot be cured by weapons only. It also requires an ideological cure," the 30-year-old says of the facility, which in many ways serves as the center-piece of Saudi Arabia's counter-terrorism strategy.

As the kingdom faces a new domestic threat from the Islamic State group that has killed 40 Saudi civilians and security personnel since November, it is revving up the groundbreaking program, which rehabilitates extremists through months of indoctrination by moderate Islamic clerics, sociologists and psychologists.

The effort is complicated by the kingdom's regional competition with Shiite rival Iran, which has stoked anti-Shiite rhetoric from hard-line Saudi clerics and fueled attacks on the country's Shiite Muslim minority, viewed by Sunni extremists like the Islamic State group as apostates.

Across the kingdom, Saudi officials and commentators slam Iran as an expansionist power that seeks to dominate the region, but conservative clerics take it even further, using language that is often laced with derogatory references to Shiites in general. In sermons and on Twitter, these clerics, who follow an ultraconservative Sunni doctrine known as Wahhabism, refer to Shiites as "rafideen," an Arabic slur for "rejectionists."

They condemn Shiite rituals, like praying at the tombs of revered figures, as an aberration of Islam and accuse Shiites of being faithful to hard-line clerics in theocratic Iran.

When 20-year-old suicide bomber Saleh bin Abdelrahman al-Qashimi unleashed the deadliest attack in the kingdom in more than a decade, targeting a Shiite mosque in eastern Saudi Arabia last month, his uncle blamed hard-line Wahhabi clerics for encouraging young men like his nephew toward extremism.

"They plant the seed in their minds," Mohammed Abdelrazzak al-Qashimi said of his nephew, who had disappeared a year before carrying out the May 22 attack, which killed 22 Shiite worshippers commemorating the birth of a revered saint.

That bombing, and an attack a week later that killed four people outside a large Shiite mosque in the eastern city of Dammam, were claimed by the Islamic State group. Residents in eastern Saudi Arabia, home to most of the country's Shiites, erected a banner with screenshots of 11 Wahhabi preachers and their anti-Shiite tweets. "These are the real killers," it read.

For many Saudi Shiites, the attacks, which began in November when eight worshippers were gunned down by alleged Islamic State militants, have come as no surprise. For nearly three years, clerics across the Gulf urged young men to join in jihad and purge Syria of its Iranian-backed government - sermons that helped draw more than 2,500 Saudis to fight alongside Sunni rebels trying to topple President Bashar Assad. That was until last year, when the kingdom decreed it illegal to fight jihad abroad or encourage it.

The Interior Ministry says around 650 fighters have since returned home, many bringing with them skills learned on foreign battlefields. So the Islamic State group changed tactics. It called on its Saudi supporters to carry out attacks inside the kingdom, which is custodian to Islam's holiest sites in Mecca and Medina.

For this new generation of home-grown extremists, the Islamic State group's ideology is attractive because its fighters are on the ground battling Iranian-backed militias in Syria and Iraq, says Abdulrahman al-Hadlaq, director of ideological security at the Interior Ministry and a founder of the rehab center.

The militant group, which was once al-Qaida in Iraq, "tricked a lot of youth," who saw them as the only force taking on the Shiite militias, he says, adding that his agency was revising its strategies to counter the dangers posed by the Islamic State group.

A key element of the kingdom's counter-terrorism arsenal is the Mohammed bin Nayef Center for Advice, Counseling and Care, as the rehab center is formally known.

Founded in 2007 by the prince whose name it bears - himself the target of several assassination attempts - its aim was the rehabilitation through religious re-education and psychological counseling of militants responsible for an earlier wave of al-Qaida bombings, shootings and kidnappings from 2003-2006.

With hundreds of militants filling up the kingdom's prisons, the center's focus was on trying to prevent those who had served their sentences from taking up arms again. It has treated some 3,000 men convicted of terrorism-related crimes, including all those released to Saudi custody from Guantanamo Bay, and claims a success rate of 87 percent.

Of the 13 percent, or roughly 390, who returned to militancy, half have been rearrested. Several turned up in Yemen to lead the local al-Qaida branch there.

Former Islamic militant, 30-year-old Badr al-Enezi, stands in a courtyard at the Mohammed bin Nayef Center for Advice, Counseling and Care in Riyadh, Saudi Arabia. The center requires al-Enezi's face not be shown due to security reasons, April 26, 2015. (AP Photo/Hasan Jamali)

At the center, inmates - called "beneficiaries" by staff - are housed in a complex of low-rise buildings, whose resort-like appearance is belied by the concrete walls, barbed wire and armed guards that surround it. Contact with family is encouraged, and participants are given access to private, fully-furnished apartments for conjugal visits with spouses.

If the center's team of experts deems an inmate mentally fit for release, they help him find a job, rent a house, buy a car and assimilate back into society.

Speaking to The Associated Press in front of psychologists at the center, al-Enezi said the program, which he completed in 2012, helped him understand religious doctrine through a different prism from what he'd learned online.

Clerics explained the Quran to him in a way that led him to believe whoever fights in jihad abroad is "serving a foreign agenda."

John Horgan, author of "The Psychology of Terrorism," says the Saudis took the idea of de-radicalization seriously and used creative techniques at a time when the West was increasingly relying on torture and drone strikes.

However, he says many see the Saudis as hypocritical when claiming moral high ground on counterterrorism efforts because they haven't prevented citizens from joining extremist groups in the first place.

"Some critics would say that this isn't true de-radicalization, this is just a diversion. It's smoke and mirrors," Horgan says. "What I've seen so far is that it's just a token gesture. It's very good for the optics and very good for public relations."

Mohammed al-Nimr, whose brother is an outspoken Saudi Shiite cleric, says changing the mindset of young men through the rehab program is not enough. An overhaul of the education system is needed as part of the counterterrorism strategy, he said.

The turn to the Islamic State group by young Saudis "is a result of the ideological terrorism that is taught in our schools," he says. "They do not teach anyone to respect people with contrary views. They use religious justification for the killing of these people."

Chapter 11

CHILDREN ARE THE FUTURE

An Islamic militant group fighter stands with two children posing with weapons as they watch other members of the group parade in commandeered Iraqi security forces vehicles down a main road at the northern city of Mosul, Iraq, more than two weeks after IS took over the country's second largest city. Across the vast region in Syria and Iraq that is part of the Islamic State group's self-declared caliphate, children are being inculcated with the extremist group's radical and violent interpretation of Shariah law, June 23, 2014. (AP Photo/Militant Website)

'DAESH HAS NOTHING TO LOSE'
Baghdad, Iraq, Wednesday, November 19, 2014

The former Islamic State group commander walked into the visitors' room of his Baghdad prison, without the usual yellow jumpsuit and shackles his fellow inmates wear. In slippers and a track suit, he greeted guards with a big smile, kissing them on the cheeks.

The scene testifies to the strange path of Abu Shakr, a 36-year-old who joined al-Qaida out of anger over treatment of Iraq's Sunnis and rose in the group as it transformed into the extremist juggernaut now called the Islamic State. Finally, he became an informant against the group after his capture.

Arrested in late 2013, he was presented a choice by Iraqi security officials: Help them against the extremists and in return he would get jailhouse perks. Now with relatively free rein inside the confines of a maximum security prison complex, Abu Shakr can play with his five children, enjoy supervised visits and buddy up with the guards.

Security officials say he has given them guidance on the extremists' tactics and helped them find, capture and interrogate suspected militants. In Salahuddin province, a key front line north of Baghdad, he helped the military win back key areas this week, including the town of Beiji, where troops secured Iraq's largest oil refinery.

He clearly has been willing to act against his former group in return for access to his family - and perhaps, implicitly, to prevent any government action against them. But his personal sentiment toward the militants is hard to gauge. Speaking to The Associated Press, he didn't express any remorse for his involvement in the group or directly denounce its actions or talk of any ideological conversion. He only said he never liked the group's ferocious targeting of Shiites and Christians. "It was not supposed to be this way," he said.

"We can't stop this thing, but we can limit it," he said of the Sunni militant group. "Daesh has nothing to lose," he added, using its Arabic acronym.

He spoke to the AP with various prison guards coming in and out of the room and with an intelligence official - with whom he works closely - present for part of the time. He spoke on condition he be identified only by his nom de guerre to protect his family. IS militants have issued numerous death threats against him.

Abu Shakr's drive to wage jihad was twofold: He said he was enraged by the U.S.-led occupation in Iraq that overthrew Saddam Hussein in 2003 and bitter toward the new Shiite-led government that Sunnis feel discriminates against them.

A graduate of Baghdad University, he joined al-Qaida's branch in Iraq in 2007. His reasoning, he said: "If we invaded America, what would be the reaction? The American people ... would resist, of course."

He said he climbed al-Qaida's ranks, starting as a foot soldier, moving from his native Diyala province to Baghdad, then to Salahuddin and finally stationed in the western city of Fallujah.

"When you get a new assignment with your company, sometimes you have to move," he said. "This was no different."

During that time, al-Qaida in Iraq's leaders - Abu Ayyub al-Masri and Abu Omar al-Baghdadi - were killed by a 2010 U.S. airstrike. They were replaced by the ambitious Abu Bakr al-Baghdadi, who would transform the group. In 2012, he began sending fighters into Syria, barging into that country's civil war. There, the group garnered battlefield prowess, resources and more fighters.

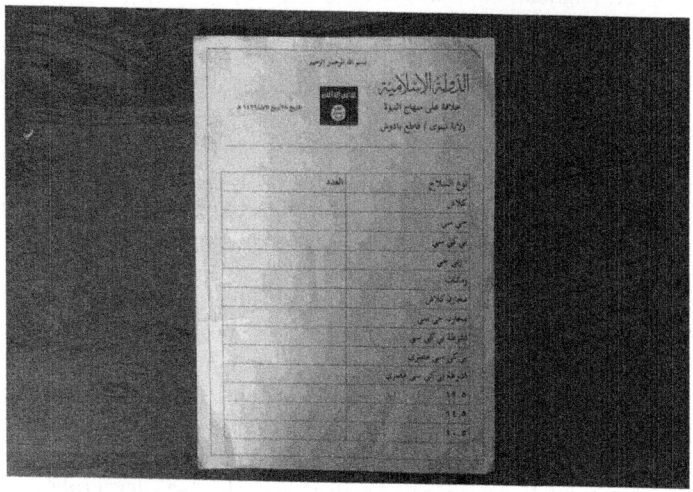

An Islamic State weapons inventory list that is kept at all headquarters across the caliphate in Mosul, Iraq, May 17, 2015. (AP Photo/Bram Janssen)

Abu Shakr was assigned to Fallujah in 2012. His task was to oversee security for al-Qaida's operations there. That meant in part organizing safehouses and movement between Iraq and Syria, but security officials said he was also responsible for Iraqi deaths from ordering militants in fighting with troops.

Fallujah fell completely to the militants in January this year, two months after Abu Shakr's arrest. But even at the time he deployed there, he said, much of the city was under the group's sway.

Their weapons were primitive at that time, he said. They could easily build explosives, he said, "but we had very few weapons. We had to rely on primitive car bombs, IEDs, as well as street fights with the army."

But they gradually drew support from Sunni tribes across Anbar province, resentful of the government. "The tribes feel the issue of oppression. For example, they didn't get a percentage of contracts ... or someone to represent them in the government," he said.

With resources from Syria, the group could provide fighters with a comfortable salary. Abu Shakr said he was getting the equivalent of $65 a month, plus an extra $45 for his wife and $20 per child.

Al-Baghdadi accelerated the group's transformation. In early 2013, the group renamed itself the Islamic State of Iraq and the Levant. It began seizing territory in Syria, leading to bloody frictions with Syrian rebels. Al-Qaida's central leader Ayman al-Zawahri began to criticize the network's Iraqi branch.

Under al-Baghdadi, "the operation changed," Abu Shakr said. Policies became "random," he said. Frictions with al-Qaida Central deepened. For example, "al-Zawahri objected to the policy of beheading. He told them, 'Don't get carried away with this publicity, it is not acceptable'," Abu Shakr said.

By the end of 2013, al-Qaida formally ejected al-Baghdadi's group. Al-Baghdadi burst forth only more powerful, first overrunning Fallujah and parts of Anbar. Then his fighters captured Iraq's second-largest city Mosul in the north in June. The group now controls around a third of Iraq and Syria.

By that point, however, Abu Shakr had been caught.

Iraqi intelligence forces had learned of his high-level role and began inquiring about him through informants around town. Haitham, an intelligence officer, said an intelligence team staked out his Fallujah home for 11 days, watching him and his family come and go. Haitham said he would even sneak into the house to listen to Abu Shakr's conversations. He spoke on condition he be identified only by his first name because he still works undercover.

Finally in late 2013, they arrested Abu Shakr. Intelligence officials worked to flip him. "Everyone has a weakness," Haitham said. "His biggest weakness is his family. ... We knew that if we were going to get him to cooperate with us, we needed to get his family too."

An Interior Ministry spokesman said Abu Shakr has not yet been sentenced for his collaboration with the radical group and the case is ongoing.

During the interview, Abu Shakr's 2-year-old daughter entered the visitor's room, her hair styled in a short bob. She greeted the guards with a bashful kiss on the cheek.

Abu Shakr says he considers the government his family's protector now. "I may be in prison for the rest of my life, and I'm sorry for that," he continued. "But I see now that it was my arrest that saved my family."

DIFFERENT WORLD OF ART AND CULTURE
Baghdad, Iraq, Thursday, November 20, 2014

Ann Khalid did not feel well but she insisted on dancing a brief scene from Tchaikovsky's Swan Lake with her classmates. The 12-year-old is determined to one day have a career dancing and teaching ballet, not an easy path in a country torn for years by conflict.

Students practice in a dancing studio at the Baghdad School of Music and Ballet in Monsur district in Baghdad, Iraq, November 12, 2014. (AP Photo/Khalid Mohammed)

"My school and my church are the two things I love the most in Baghdad," the soft-spoken Khalid, in her black leotard and white ballet shoes, said with pride after the dance.

If she has a shot at her dream, it's because of the Baghdad School of Music and Ballet.

The school has managed to survive decades of turmoil, a feat that speaks to the resilience of Baghdad's residents through war after war. The Iraqi capital's past as a Middle East center of culture is a distant memory, but the school has carved out a tiny island of creativity amid the violence that is an inescapable part of daily life and the religious conservatism that now defines public life.

"Where else in Iraq can you walk into a school and listen to a small boy playing Antonio Vivaldi on his violin?" boasts the school principal, Ahmed Salim Ghani, himself a virtuoso player of the contrabass and the oud, an Arab instrument resembling the lute.

Another rarity: It isn't segregated by sex like almost all Iraqi schools. Male and female students take classes together from kindergarten to high school.

"The second you walk through the gate, you find yourself in a different world, one of art and culture," Ghani said.

Ghani proudly declares himself a "genuine" Baghdadi. He speaks nostalgically about Baghdad's golden age - the 1960s through to the 1980s. Back then, the city's elite patronized art and culture, while deeply secular, albeit dictatorial, regimes ensured that enough of the nation's petrodollars went to the arts. The school, founded in 1968, thrived.

Black-and-white footage of a 1977 school production of The Nutcracker shows a relatively high level of discipline, with the children dancing in professional-level costumes. In class photos from the era, the schoolgirls and female teachers wear miniskirts. The boys wear blazers and bow ties.

Things rapidly worsened for Baghdad and the school with Iraq's 1990 invasion of Kuwait. U.N. sanctions devastated the economy, ruptured the nation's social fabric and forced hundreds of thousands to leave their homes in rural areas. They descended on the city to find work, bringing with them the conservative traditions of their villages.

With state coffers emptying, Russian instructors brought to the Baghdad school were sent home.

The city plunged deeper into chaos after the 2003 U.S.-led invasion. The school was looted days after Saddam Hussein's ouster. Later it was partially burned during a rampage by disgruntled Saddam-era officers.

Amid the violence, religious extremism rose, nurturing the notion that ballet - and to a lesser extent music - is immoral and anti-Islamic.

The school removed its large street sign to escape attention. Children hid their musical instruments when out in public or left them at school. Some of the policemen assigned to protect the building asked for transfers, not wanting to be associated with an "immoral" institution.

Daily bombings, assassinations and kidnappings forced parents to keep their children at home. The school's best Iraqi ballet and music teachers fled, seeking employment abroad. During the height of the violence, in the mid-2000s, the number of students plunged to an all-time low of 100-120, according to Ghani.

Security in the city has improved, but bombings continue.

"We hope it is just a phase that will eventually go away," said Salam Arab, whose 16-year-old son Maysara is considered one of the school's best male dancers. "It's a rare school in the Arab world, and it is very important that it continues to carry out its mission."

Students practice in a music studio at the Baghdad School of Music and Ballet, November 12, 2014. (AP Photo/Khalid Mohammed)

The conservative religiosity that pervades Baghdad's society has a powerful effect as well.

The school now has around 500 students. But many parents now pull their daughters out of ballet when they are 12 or 13 because they object on religious grounds to the girls being lifted and embraced by boys their age while performing, according to Zeina Akram Fayzy, a 40-year-old ballet instructor.

"Years of our hard work go to waste," lamented Fayzy, an alumna of the school. "The school needs talented children who stay the course."

Leezan Salam, who graduated this year, said that when she started ballet at the school, there were around 30 girls with her. By the time she reached 10th grade, "we were only three."

"The future of ballet in Iraq is dismal. No one really cares," said Salam, 18, a lanky brunette with a dreamy voice. She now teaches children while pursuing her own dance career, hoping to perform solo.

Khalid, the 12-year-old, says the moral questions surrounding dance don't dent her enthusiasm.

"Everyone says it is haram (religiously prohibited) and disgraceful. But my parents are happy for me to dance," she said. She's the daughter of artistic parents - her father is an actor and her mother a television director.

Dance can be equally problematic for boys.

Maysara said he doesn't tell people he dances. "Those in my neighborhood who have found out often mock me," he said.

As they did drills together, his fellow dancer Moayed Nawar interjected, "I want to dance professionally."

Then the 13-year-old added defiantly, "I am not going to stop, stay home and shut up about it."

CHILD SOLDIERS
Beirut, Lebanon, Monday, November 24, 2014

Teenagers carrying weapons stand at checkpoints and busy intersections in Iraq's second-largest city, Mosul. Patched onto the left arms of their black uniforms are the logos of the Islamic Police.

In Raqqa, the Islamic State group's de facto capital in Syria, boys attend training camp and religious courses before heading off to fight. Others serve as cooks or guards at the extremists' headquarters or as spies, informing on people in their neighborhoods.

Across the vast region under IS control, the group is actively conscripting children for battle and committing abuses against the most vulnerable at a young age, according to a growing body of evidence assembled from residents, activists, independent experts and human rights groups.

In the northern Syrian town of Kobani, where ethnic Kurds have been resisting an IS onslaught for weeks, several activists told The Associated Press they observed children fighting alongside the militants. Mustafa Bali, a Kobani-based activist, said he saw the bodies of four boys, two of them younger than 14. And at least one 18 year old is said to have carried out a suicide attack.

In Syria's Aleppo province, an activist affiliated with the rebel Free Syrian Army said its fighters encountered children in their late teens "fairly often" in battles against the rival Islamic State group.

It is difficult to determine just how widespread the exploitation of children is in the closed world of IS-controlled territory. There are no reliable figures on the number of minors the group employs.

Young Shiite volunteer militia members prepare to attack Islamic State fighters in Tikrit, north of Baghdad. The Associated Press has found that militia forces battling the Islamic State group are actively training children under 18 years old, March 15, 2015. (AP Photo/Khalid Mohammed)

Young boys known as the "lion cubs" hold rifles and Islamic State group flags as they exercise at a training camp in Tal Afar, near Mosul, northern Iraq, April 25, 2015. (AP Photo/Militant Website)

However, a video posted on militant websites Monday offered the most substantive evidence to date that the militant group enlists children. It purportedly highlights the so-called "Cubs of the Caliphate" class, showing young children dressed in black training to use different weapons, responding to staged ambushes and learning to manufacture explosives. The video corresponded with AP reporting.

But a United Nations panel investigating war crimes in the Syrian conflict concluded that in its enlistment of children for active combat roles, the Islamic State group is perpetrating abuses and war crimes on a massive scale "in a systematic and organized manner."

The group "prioritizes children as a vehicle for ensuring long-term loyalty, adherence to their ideology and a cadre of devoted fighters that will see violence as a way of life," it said in a recent report. The panel of experts, known as the Independent International Commission of Inquiry on Syria, conducted more than 300 interviews with people who fled or are living in IS-controlled areas, and examined video and photographic evidence.

The use of children by armed groups in conflict is, of course, nothing new. In the Syrian civil war, the Free Syrian Army and Nusra Front rebel groups also recruit children for combat, said

Leila Zerrougui, the U.N. secretary-general's special representative for children and armed conflict.

But no other group comes close to IS in using children in such a systematic and organized way. And the effect is that much greater because IS commands large areas in which the militants inculcate the children with their radical and violent interpretation of Shariah law.

"What is new is that ISIS seems to be quite transparent and vocal about their intention and their practice of recruiting children," said Laurent Chapuis, UNICEF regional child protection adviser for the Middle East and North Africa, using an alternate acronym for the group. "Children as young as 10, 12 years old are being used in a variety of roles, as combatants as messengers, spies, guards, manning checkpoints but also for domestic purposes like cooking, cleaning, sometimes providing medical care to the wounded."

"This is not a marginal phenomenon. This is something that is being observed and seems to be part of the strategy of the group," Zerrougui said in a phone interview from New York.

She said some children join voluntarily for various reasons but others are targeted.

"They are abducting children and forcing them to join, they are brainwashing children and indoctrinating them to join their group. All the tools used to attract and recruit children are used by this group," she said, adding that children as young as 9 or 10 are used for "various roles."

In areas of Syria and Iraq under their control, the Sunni extremists have closed schools or changed the curriculum to fit with their ideology. Their goal, according to the U.N., is to use education as a tool of indoctrination to foster a new generation of supporters.

A video recently published by an IS media arm shows what it says is a graduation ceremony for boys, who appear to be in their teens. Dressed in military uniforms, they are lined up to shake hands with a sheikh. Another scene shows the boys posing with AK-47s, their faces hidden under black masks. The video touts the children as a "generation of lions, protectors of religion, dignity and land."

Residents of IS-controlled areas said the militants are teaching children at school to become fighters.

A young Shiite volunteer militiaman stands near a vehicle on his way to the battlefield against Islamic State fighters in Tikrit, Iraq, March 15, 2015. (AP Photo/Khalid Mohammed)

One resident in the Iraqi city of Fallujah described seeing his 6-year-old son playing with a water pistol in front of the house and screaming: "I am a fighter for the Islamic State!"

"I waved him to come to me and I broke the gun in two pieces," said the man, who spoke on condition of anonymity out of fear of his life.

He also said he and his son recently stopped at an IS checkpoint. His son shouted, "We love the State!" and one of the fighters asked, "Which state?" When the son replied, "the Islamic State," the fighter "told him, 'Good boy,' and let us through," the resident said. The incident persuaded the man to move his family to the northern city of Kirkuk, now in Kurdish hands.

"The boys are studying, not to learn, but to become mujahedeen," he said.

Earlier this year in Syria, the Islamic State group abducted more than 150 Kurdish boys, held them in a school in Aleppo province and showed them videos of beheadings and attacks, while subjecting them to daily instruction on militant ideology for five months, the U.N. and Kurdish officials said. The boys were later released.

Militants of the Islamic State group hold up their weapons and wave its flags on their vehicles in a convoy on a road leading to Iraq, while riding in Raqqa city in Syria, (AP Photo/Militant Website)

In Raqqa province, an anti-IS activist collective has documented the presence of at least five known youth training camps, one specifically for children under 16 in the town of Tabqa. The collective, named Raqqa is Being Slaughtered Silently, has released a video showing children crawling under barbed wire as part of their military training. The video could not be independently confirmed but is consistent with AP reporting on the subject.

Residents in IS-controlled areas in Iraq, such as Mosul and Fallujah, say it is not uncommon to see gun-toting boys in their late teens standing at checkpoints and even younger ones riding in militant convoys, usually accompanying their fathers in parades.

Another resident of Fallujah said many boys as young as 11 volunteer to join the group, but that IS often seeks the parents' consent for those under 16. He said others join under pressure or in exchange for money.

"Once they're done training, their skills and abilities are tested before they decide where to send them off. Many want to be on the front lines," said the man, who identified himself as Abu Abdullah al-Falluji.

In a report released earlier this year, Human Rights Watch interviewed four former IS child fighters in Syria who described military training with the group. One, Bassem, who joined the group at 16, said he left after being seriously wounded by shrapnel in battle. A 17 year old, Amr, told the group that children in his unit signed up for suicide missions - and that he reluctantly did so as well under pressure.

Thousands of foreign fighters have flocked to IS areas from all over the world, many of them with their families.

A video emerged this month showing two boys, both speaking perfect French, holding guns aloft and claiming to be in Raqqa. They stand on a dusty street; a man walks by and takes no notice of their weapons. The boys, who look much younger than 10, say they're from Strasbourg and Toulouse. French prosecutors have opened a formal investigation to identify the children.

"Over there, you're in a country of infidels. Here, we're mujahedeen. We're in Syria, we're in Raqqa here," one of the boys says in the video. "It's war here."

Chapter 12

CHRONOLOGY

Croatia's prime minister Zoran Milanovic attends a press conference in Zagreb, Croatia. Islamic State sympathizers circulated an image that appears to show the grisly aftermath of the beheading of Tomislav Salopek, a Croatian hostage abducted in Egypt, which if confirmed would mark the first such killing of a foreign captive in the country since the extremist group established a branch here last year, August 12, 2015. (AP Photo/Goran Stanzl)

HISTORY OF THE ISLAMIC STATE GROUP
Cairo, Egypt, Wednesday, August 12, 2015

An online image released Wednesday purported to show the Islamic State affiliate in Egypt had beheaded a Croatian hostage.

Here's a look at the Islamic State group's birth, its atrocities and the world's response to the extremists:

April 18, 2010 - U.S. and Iraqi forces kill two top al-Qaida in Iraq leaders, allowing Abu Bakr al-Baghdadi to become the leader of a terror group weakened by a concerted campaign aimed at ending a Sunni insurgency in the country. The organization later would become the Islamic State group.

October 31, 2010 - Al-Baghdadi's al-Qaida militants attack Our Lady of Salvation Catholic church in Baghdad during Sunday night mass, killing 58 people in the deadliest assault targeting Christians since the 2003 U.S.-led invasion there. The militants reportedly demand the release of Muslim women they claim were held by Egypt's Coptic Christian church.

October 4, 2011 - The U.S. puts a $10 million bounty on al-Baghdadi's head over a series of attacks he orchestrated.

July 21, 2012 - In his first purported online message, al-Baghdadi promises to regain lost ground in Iraq and calls on militants to "chase and liquidate the judges, the investigators and the guards." Within days, his group begins a campaign of attacks, car bombings and other assaults killing hundreds. He also mentions Syria, in the grips of a civil war pitting largely Sunni rebels against embattled President Bashar Assad. By this time, al-Baghdadi already has begun to send fighters there.

April 2013 - Al-Baghdadi announces his group has taken over the Nusra Front, the al-Qaida affiliate in Syria. Nusra denies the takeover, sparking anger and infighting that continues to this day.

July 2013 - A military-style assault by al-Baghdadi's fighters on two Baghdad-area prisons free more than 500 inmates.

January 2014 - Al-Baghdadi's forces sweep into Ramadi and Fallujah in Iraq's Anbar province, which Iraqi security forces had abandoned weeks earlier. That came after security forces killed demonstrators during a Sunni protest, effectively turning the unrest into an uprising.

Early February 2014 - Al-Qaida breaks with al-Baghdadi's group, now known as the Islamic State of Iraq and the Levant. Al-Baghdadi ignores al-Qaida as his group now has control of wide regions of Syria, including the city of Raqqa, which becomes the group's de facto capital.

June 10, 2014 - Al-Baghdadi's fighters take over Iraq's second-largest city of Mosul, followed by Saddam Hussein's hometown of Tikrit and smaller communities in the Sunni heartland as government forces melt away.

June 29, 2014 - The group declares the establishment of an Islamic state, or caliphate, in territories it controls in Iraq and Syria and demands allegiance from Muslims worldwide. It declares al-Baghdadi the leader of the new caliphate. The militants rename themselves the Islamic State group.

July 5, 2104 - A man purporting to be al-Baghdadi makes his first public appearance, delivering a sermon at a mosque in Mosul.

August 8 - The U.S. begins targeting the Islamic State group with airstrikes, citing the humanitarian plight of Iraq's minorities, like the Yazidi.

August 19 - The Islamic State group releases a video showing a jihadi behead James Foley, a 40-year-old journalist from Rochester, New Hampshire, in response to the U.S.-led airstrikes. This marks the first of many videos showing militants behead Western captives.

September 2 - The Islamic State group releases a video showing a jihadi behead American-Israeli journalist Steven Sotloff.

September 13 - The Islamic State group releases a video showing a jihadi behead British aid worker David Haines.

October 3 - The Islamic State group releases a video showing a jihadi behead British hostage Alan Henning.

November 8 - Iraqi officials say al-Baghdadi is wounded in an airstrike on an Iraqi town near the Syrian border. Days later, an online audio message purportedly from al-Baghdadi urges his followers to "explode the volcanoes of jihad everywhere."

November 16 - An Islamic State group video shows extremists behead a dozen Syrian soldiers and U.S. aid worker Peter Kassig.

January 10 - An online video shows Taliban fighters in Pakistan pledge loyalty to the Islamic State group and behead a man they identify as a soldier. Similar pledges previously arose from Egypt, Yemen and elsewhere in the Mideast. Afghan authorities later acknowledge a similar presence in their country.

January 24 - A message claims the Islamic State group beheads Japanese hostage Haruna Yukawa, a 42-year-old adventurer, after earlier demanding $200 million for him and captive Japanese journalist Kenji Goto. Japanese and Jordanian officials attempt to negotiate a prisoner swap to free him and captured Jordanian pilot 1st Lieutenant Mu'ath al-Kaseasbeh.

January 26 - Kurdish fighters take control of the Syrian border town of Kobani near Turkey after fighting the Islamic State group for months. U.S.-led airstrikes helped turn the tide for the Kurds.

January 31 - The Islamic State group releases a video saying it beheaded Goto.

February 3 - The Islamic State group releases a video of it burning al-Kaseasbeh to death in a cage, sparking outrage in Jordan, which launches new strikes targeting the militants.

February 6 - The Islamic State group claims a Jordanian airstrike kills American hostage Kayla Jean Mueller. U.S. officials later confirm her death, but say it wasn't caused by a Jordanian airstrike.

February 15 - Libyan militants who earlier pledged their loyalty to the Islamic State group behead a group of Coptic Christians from Egypt in an online video.

February 16 - Egypt launches airstrikes in Libya in retaliation for the beheadings.

March 11 - After days of besieging Tikrit, Iraqi troops and allied Shiite militiamen enter the Islamic State-held city, backed by Iranian advisers and forgoing the air support of the U.S.-led coalition.

March 20 - A group identifying itself as an affiliate of the Islamic State group in Yemen claims a series of suicide bombings killing 137 people and wounding 345, though U.S. officials express skepticism about the claim.

March 25 - The U.S.-led coalition begins airstrikes on Tikrit after Iraqi efforts to take the city stall. Shiite militias pull out of Iraqi forces in protest, but later rejoin the offensive.

April 1 - Iraq declares a "magnificent victory" over the Islamic State group in Tikrit, its biggest gain yet against the militants.

April 18 - Afghan President Ashraf Ghani blames the Islamic State group for a suicide bombing in the country that kills at least 35 people and wounds 125.

April 19 - Islamic State affiliates in Libya release a video showing them behead and shoot dead groups of Ethiopian Christians, slayings resembling the February beheadings of the Egyptian Coptic Christians.

May 17 - The contested Iraqi city of Ramadi falls to the Islamic State group as Iraqi forces abandon their weapons and armored vehicles to flee the provincial capital in a major loss despite intensified U.S.-led airstrikes.

June 16 - Kurds take crucial Syrian border town of Tal Abyad from Islamic State group.

July 23 - Turkey agrees to let the United States launch airstrikes against the Islamic State group from its strategic Incirlik Air Base. Turkey later begins striking Islamic State targets in Syria, as well as Kurdish forces it considers threats.

August 5 - An affiliate of the Islamic State group threatens to kill Croatian hostage Tomislav Salopek in 48 hours unless Egypt releases "Muslim women" it holds in prison.

August 12 - An online image purports to show Salopek beheaded by the Islamic State affiliate in Egypt.

CITATIONS AND BYLINES

Introduction
ISIS, ISIL, DAESH, ISLAMIC STATE?
Baghdad, Friday, September 12, 2014
By Vivian Salama

Chapter 1. Nation of Fear
HOW ISLAMIC IS THE ISLAMIC STATE? NOT VERY
Cairo, Monday, March 2, 2015
By Lee Keath and Hamza Hendawi
BRUTAL PEOPLE
Eski Mosul, Iraq, Thursday, June 18, 2015
By Zeina Karam, Vivian Salama, Bram Janssen, and Lee Keath
SAVED BY CIGARETTES
Eski Mosul, Iraq, Sunday, June 21, 2015
By Vivian Salama and Bram Janssen

Chapter 2. Inside the Caliphate
CARROT AND STICK
Beirut, Lebanon, Thursday, November 27, 2014
By Ryan Lucas
PAID HONEYMOON
Beirut, Lebanon, Tuesday, May 26, 2015
By Sarah el Deeb
WATER AS A WEAPON
Baghdad, Iraq, Thursday, June 4, 2015
By Sameer N. Yacoub
TWO FACES OF ISLAMIC STATE
Beirut, Lebanon, Friday, July 10, 2015
By Hamza Hendawi and Bassem-Mroue

Chapter 3. Behead the Doll
FIGHT TO THE DEATH
Baghdad, Iraq, Wednesday, July 8, 2015
By Hamza Hendawi, Qassim Abdul-Zahra, and Bassem-Mroue
BEHEAD THE DOLL
Sanliurfa, Turkey, Monday, July 20, 2015
By Zeina Karam and Bram Janssen
SUMMER CAMP IN IRAQ
Baghdad, Iraq, Tuesday, July 28, 2015
By Vivian Salama and Qassim Abdul-Zahra

Chapter 4. Fight, or Flight?
RAMADI GHOST TOWN
Baghdad, Iraq, Thursday, April 16, 2015
By Sameer N. Yacoub
THE BZEBIZ BRIDGE

On the Bzebiz Bridge, Iraq, Tuesday, April 21, 2015
By Vivian Salama

Chapter 5. Stranger Than Fiction
REMOVING WOMEN FROM PUBLIC LIFE
Beirut, Lebanon, Tuesday, December 23, 2014
By Zeina Karam
A NOT SO GREAT CALIPHATE
Baghdad, Iraq, Saturday, December 13, 2014
By Sameer N. Yacoub and Vivian Salama
IRAQI REALITY TV
Baghdad, Iraq, Monday, December 22, 2014
By Vivian Salama
SHIITE FIGHTERS
Baghdad, Iraq, Saturday, December 20, 2014
By Sameer N. Yacoub and Sinan Salaheddin
GHOST SOLDIERS
Baghdad, Iraq, Tuesday, December 16, 2014
By Qassim Abdul Zahra and Vivian Salama

Chapter 6. Media Wars
GLOSSY MAGAZINES AND SLICK SOCIAL MEDIA
Dubai, United Arab Emirates, Sunday, September 21, 2014
By Aya Batrawy
INSPIRING TERRORISM
New York, Sunday, September 21, 2014
By Tom Hays
BRITISH JIHADIS
Portsmouth, England, Tuesday, November 4, 2014
By Gregory Katz
TONE SOUNDS MUCH LIKE NPR
Paris, France, Monday, June 1, 2015
By Lori Hinnant

Chapter 7. Captive
'WHERE IS GOD?'
Dahuk, Iraq, Friday, October 3, 2014
By Vivian Salama
SOLD AS A SLAVE
Maqluba, Iraq, Saturday, October 11, 2014
By Dalton Bennett
HARD LINE INTERPRETATION OF ISLAM
Baghdad, Iraq, Sunday, October 12, 2014
By Vivian Salama
ENDURING HORRORS AT THE HANDS OF THE ISLAMIC STATE
Baghdad, Iraq, Tuesday, December 23, 2014
By Sinan Salaheddin

Chapter 8. The Allure of the Islamic State
JIHADS LEGIONNAIRES
Pankisi Gorge, Georgia, Thursday, May 21, 2015
By John-Thor Dahlburg and Misha Dzhindzhikhashvili
DEATH ON A SYRIAN BATTLEFIELD
Rabat, Morocco, Thursday, May 21, 2015
By Paul Schemm
LOOKING FOR PARADISE
Minneapolis, Thursday, May 21, 2015
By Amy Forliti
SPECIALLY DESIGNATED GLOBAL TERRORIST
Birkiani, Georgia, Thursday, May 21, 2015
By Misha Dzhindzhikhashvili
MARTYRDOM OPERATIONS VOLUNTEER
Amman, Jordan, Sunday, October 4, 2015
By Hamza al-Soud

Chapter 9. Women of the Islamic State
'FALSE HEAVEN'
Istanbul, Wednesday, September 24, 2014
By Berza Simsek and Raphael Satter
LURED BY THE ISLAMIC STATE
Washington, D. C., Tuesday, December 16, 2014
By Eric Tucker and Sadie Gurman
MARTYRDOM, 'A GIRL CAN ONLY WISH'
Philadelphia, Friday, April 3, 2015
By Maryclaire Dale
AUSTRALIAN BRIDE
Canberra, Australia, Sunday, May 21, 2015
By Rod McGuirk
MANY REASONS FOR JOINING THE ISLAMIC STATE
London, Thursday, May 28, 2015
By Danica Kirka

Chapter 10. Coming Home
HOME FROM JIHAD
Maan, Jordan, Saturday, December 6, 2014
By Karin Laub and Mohammed Daraghmeh
EXTREMISTS BIDING THEIR TIME
Maan, Jordan, Saturday, December 6, 2014
By Mohammed Daraghmeh and Karin Laub
RECRUITS FROM THE WEST
Berlin, Wednesday, June 3, 2015
By Frank Jordans
DE-RADICALIZING JIHADISTS
Riyadh, Saudi Arabia, Wednesday, June 24, 2015
By Aya Batrawy

Chapter 11. Children are the Future
'DAESH HAS NOTHING TO LOSE'
Baghdad, Iraq, Wednesday, November 19, 2014
By Vivian Salama

DIFFERENT WORLD OF ART AND CULTURE
Baghdad, Iraq, Thursday, November 20, 2014
By Hamza Hendawi
CHILD SOLDIERS
Beirut, Lebanon, Monday, November 24, 2014
By Zeina Karam and Vivian Salama

Chapter 12. Chronology
HISTORY OF THE ISLAMIC STATE GROUP
Cairo, Egypt, Wednesday, August 12, 2015
By Jon Gambrell

THE AP EMERGENCY RELIEF FUND

When Hurricane Katrina hit the Gulf Coast in 2005, many Associated Press staffers and their families were personally affected. AP employees rallied to help these colleagues by setting up the AP Emergency Relief Fund, which has become a source of crucial assistance for the past 10 years.

Established as an independent 501(c)(3), the Fund helps AP staffers who have suffered damage or losses as a result of conflict or natural disasters. These grants are used to rebuild homes, move to safe houses and repair and replace bomb-damaged belongings.

The AP matches all gifts in full and also donates the net proceeds from AP Essentials, AP's company store, to the Fund.

HOW TO GIVE

In order to be ready to help the moment emergencies strike, the Fund relies on the generous and ongoing support of the extended AP community. All donations are matched in full by The Associated Press and can be made any time at http://www.ap.org/relieffund and are tax deductible.

On behalf of the AP staffers and families who receive aid in times of crisis, the AP Emergency Relief Fund Directors and Officers thank you.

AP

ALSO AVAILABLE FROM AP EDITIONS